GOD'S TRUTH REVEALED

JULIANA F. SABAT

GOD'S
TRUTH
REVEALED

JULIANA F. SABAT

CITI OF
BOOKS

CITIOFBOOKS, INC.
3736 Eubank NE Suite A1
Albuquerque, NM 87111-3579
www.citiofbooks.com
Hotline: 1 (877) 389-2759
Fax: 1 (505) 930-7244

Ordering Information:

Quantity sales. Special discounts are available on quantity purchases by corporations, associations, and others. For details, contact the publisher at the address above.

Printed in the United States of America.

ISBN-13:   Softcover   978-1-959682-51-6
                      eBook   978-1-959682-52-3
Library of Congress Control Number: 2022922632

TABLE OF CONTENTS

"But the word of the LORD endures forever"
1 Peter 1:25

For a divine attribute of love, faith and hope, the Jackson family - Emmarie & Steven and their children, Dominique and Sofia, will always put to remembrance His precious teachings and blessings.

ABOUT THE AUTHOR

For ten years, I have devoted myself to listening to the Shepherd's Chapel on the air. In the beginning, I was "on the fence" of Pastor Arnold Murray's lessons about the Bible. After a few months of daily listening, I channeled my focus on learning from the church, and I became more devoted to studying about God.

At first, I found myself switching to different religious programs and realized that they are not beneficial because many of them contain more of the "entertaining" element, drawing more attention by including religious interaction, stories, and pictures of travel in the Middle East, and showing celebrities with their talent of religious songs and music performances, etc. I did not feel that these methods nof learning were serious r real. Then, I found myself going back to the Shepherd's Chapel, which soon became a habit. I started to tune into The Shepherd's Chapel daily. When I got to sit down to relax after my daily chores, I realized I was guided by the Holy Spirit to do so, because I found it interesting. I was more influenced to study the Bible privately.

Before my knowledge about the truth of God became broad, I read many of their books from their library by requesting materials through mthe mail. I studied seriously searching for the "Truth." I had a previous background after getting married, as my late husband and his family were Christian believers. My father-in-law was a minister of a Christian church, but worshippers failed to learn about the first "world/earth age."

Today, after learning on my own, when I compare my knowledge of God to what I've known in the past, I can boldly say that I have the true gospel armor of God like a "winner" of God's truth.

I am a grandmother who, in my little way, would like to share my God-given knowledge and wisdom to families, if not to preach today on earth, it could be instrumental to teach for tomorrow's millennium, The Day of the Lord.

I am deeply and graciously thankful to our Father in heaven for giving me strength, courage, and faith to acquire this precious gift of accomplishment from Him. I am also grateful He gave me a wonderful daughter Emmarie, (and, of course, her family, Steve, her husband, and their children, Dominique and Sofia), who have been supporting me with inspiration to write this book.

Our wonderful Father is above all to be praised with foremost credit, for He made everything possible for me to be successful.

My main goal for this project is to spread the Word of God. I pray that whoever may read this book will be blessed, as I believe His Word will light up and open the minds of those who were not learned enough to overall understand God's Word.

I give credit to The Shepherd's Chapel that made my writing possible because of their faithful service in leadership and guidance, thus, I became "polished" with God's teachings. The Father, the Son, and the Holy Spirit, above all, are appreciated. If we are obedient and do God's way, His reward is eternal life!

I am a Registered Nurse in New York. I have had an extensive practice of bedside nursing in medical institutions like Montefiore Medical Center, Beth Israel Hospital, Lincoln Hospital and Rochester Medical Hospital in New York. Besides that, I was a clinical nurse in Geriatrics for one year. I also had a private special nursing on some occasions and a foreign nursing experience in the Netherlands for year, and lastly at The University of Texas Medical Branch in my early nursing job.

I learned so much about various kinds of people dealing with sickness, physical pain, anxiety and emotional behaviors. I got involved with compassion for my patients and became concerned not only about physical care but also about the patients' spiritual care.

When I retired from my job in 1987, I studied The Bible with much concentration, so I was able to write this book with much settled peace of mind and gladness.

> *"For God giveth to a man that is good in his sight wisdom, and knowledge, and joy: but to the sinner he giveth travail, to gather and to heap up, that he may give to him that is good before God. This also is vanity and vexation of spirit." (Ecclesiastes 2:26)*

God is pleased to help you about His blessings through righteous works and be successful with your goals.

> *"For God so loved the world, that He gave His only begotten Son that whoever believes in Him should not perish but have everlasting life." (John 3:16)*

God is aware of the weaknesses of the flesh, and as a sinner, Jesus Christ became our hope. Because of God's grace through His Son with the faith working through love, we can be forgiven of our sins through repentance.

"Watch and pray, lest you enter into temptation. The spirit indeed is willing, but the flesh is weak." (Matthew 26:41)

Its works are sinful. There is no law against the works of the Spirit which are love, peace, joy, long suffering, kindness, goodness, and faithfulness.

PREFACE

The contents of this book are an overall positive and negative balance of issues between God's righteousness and Satan's evil deeds. It will show that there are two things that need to be cleared up in the minds of the readers:

1.   There are two kinds of bodies—terrestrial and celestial.

2.   There are two kinds of death—death of the flesh and death of the soul.

3.   There are two kinds of resurrection—the first resurrection and the second resurrection.

4.   There are two kinds of Jesus Christ—the true and the false.

5.   There are two kinds of tribulations—Satan's and Jesus Christ's.

6.   There are two kinds of souls—mortal and immortal.

All that is written and mentioned above will be explained in their corresponding chapters where they belong. The most important thing to remember about learning the Word of God is not to be misled by false teachings (traditions of man), as it surely leads to the pathway of Satan's doctrine. His number is 666, in which he appears at the 6th seal, the 6th trumpet, and the 6th vial. He always wants to be first, or ahead of Jesus Christ, whose number is 777.

The goal of this book is to make everyone aware of God's words, as He would like to convey to all in plain words that make it easy to understand His message: to know the history and events that happened in the beginning because they will likely happen again during the end times.

> *"I have foretold you all things. All warnings by Jesus and His apostles about deception were foretold." (Matthew 24:25)*

While we are in the flesh body, remember that Christ has not arrived yet. Do not believe anyone who tells you "look here!" or "there is Christ!" for false prophets or false Christs will arise to deceive. We must wait for our Lord Jesus Christ, when He appears at the last (seventh) trump, when everything will be changed into a spiritual body.

Above all, a wonderful and extremely beautiful kingdom of God will be put up on earth for all who overcome the trials. At that time an exciting wedding, or marriage, of Jesus Christ will take place.

The mysteries of God are revealed.

All of God's quoted words are indicated with references from the King James version of the Bible.

Some Hebrew words written can be checked out from the manuscript. A glossary page can be found at the back of this book for meanings of some words.

Other References:

1. The New Exhausted Strong's Concordance by James Strong
2. The Companion Bible by E.W. Bullinger
3. The Smiths Bible Dictionary by William Smith
4. Dr. Arnold Murray from The Shepherd's Chapel

GOD

There is no other great name that could dominate or equal the power of God.

GOD is the Creator of everything. He is our Father in heaven who made everything in heaven and earth. That is how great and incredible is the power He has. He spoke and made all things out of nothing. He speaks, and nothing can become something. He has a name called in Hebrew, ELOHIM. When He was speaking with His angels, He said, "Let us make men in our image, according to our likeness. Let them have dominion over the fish of the sea, over the birds of the air, and over the cattle, over all the earth, and over all creeping things that creep on the earth." So, He created man in His own image. He created them male and female, and blessed them and said, "Be fruitful and multiply: fill the earth." During the time of Moses, when God asked Moses to lead the children of the Hebrews to help them get out of Egyptian bondage or slavery, Moses was hesitant at first. However, after a while of talking with God, Moses asked God, "What name shall I tell them sent me to you?" God answered, "I AM. I AM THAT I AM has sent me to you" (Exodus 3:15). The divine Hebrew name of God is Jehovah, but since there is no letter "J" in Hebrew, it alone is pronounced "Ya-ho-vah," and it is written: YHVH. In short, His name is YAH (Psalms 68:4). The other name in English is LORD. "Hear, O Israel, the Lord our God is one."

"I am the Alpha and Omega, the Beginning and the End "says the "Almighty "(Revelation 1:8)

God is Holy and perfect. He is supernatural. He is loving and understanding, and possesses the Holy Spirit with great qualities of: wisdom, power, riches, strength, honor, glory, and blessings (Revelation 5:12). His laws are His teachings: the Ten Commandments, the Levitical Book, and the Deuteronomy Book, which contain His teachings to be observed and to be followed. He teaches us to be righteous, and to avoid trouble, and not to hurt ourselves, to be healthy and strong by eating the right kinds of food by eating clean animals as approved by Him, and to avoid the wrong choice of foods that are not approved by God. We achieve success with our goals of life as we practice obedience to God.

From His Ten Commandments He declared, "Thou shall have no other gods before Me." He expects us to worship Him and no other gods. We are to love and worship Him alone because He is a jealous God.

Our Father is loving and merciful, because He is aware that we are weak in the flesh in resisting temptations and are easily swayed by the wicked, so He sent His one and only begotten Son to the world for our salvation. He also makes clear about His warnings.

> *"He is a Jealous God." (Deut. 4:24). He also stated… "He is a Consuming Fire." (Exodus 20:5 & Hebrew 12:29)*

Being a powerful Creator of everything, He created us for His pleasure (Revelation 4:11). He wants our love, and He wants us to be faithful to Him. His love will give us His Holy Spirit that guides, protects, and blesses.

GOD'S LOVE AND PROMISES

1. Forgiveness through Christ – there is no person on earth who is perfect. All are considered sinners. Faith is very important, it makes us believe in God. We have as Abraham who is blessed with the promise that in Jesus Christ's repentance and forgiveness, the law of faith is working with the grace of Jesus Christ bringing us closer to God for our salvation.

2. Faith in God, and faith in the promises to Continue

Examples: Promise of God to Abraham: "And I will make of thee a great nation, and I will bless thee, and make thy name great; and thou shalt be a blessing:

> And I will bless them that bless thee, and curse him thatcurseth thee: and in thee shall all families of the earth be blessed." (Genesis 12:2-3)

THE DISCIPLINE OF GOD

God is a disciplinarian. In Jesus Christs' ministry, He taught His disciples with God's truth.

If you love God, you must love Him sincerely. He gives you free will, but if you are unrighteous, remember there are consequences to follow, especially at judgment time.

"Children, obey your parents in the Lord, for this is right. Honor your mother and father, which is the first commandment with promise that it may be well with you and you may live long on earth." (Ephesians 6:1-3)

Promise of longer life is achieved as long as you follow God's law because this is the whole duty of man, to keep His commandments, and ordinances through the sacrifice of His precious body and blood.

"As many as I love, I rebuke and chasten, therefore, be zealous and repent." (Revelation 3:19)

By nature, the flesh is weak to resist temptation, and sometimes we become unrighteous. God tells us to repent, to be forgiven, and make things right from being wrong.

GOD'S LOVE

"God is love." (1 John 4:16)

With the love of God, He gives blessings in all forms: it could be in answered prayers, petitions, or favors requested in prayers according to His will. God's rewards for being righteous and obedient to Him are blessings to be given as He promised.

Besides all the perfect and powerful descriptions written in the Bible about God, He also has emotions! He uses the word "mercy" for love and compassion.

"I desire mercy [your love] and not sacrifice and the knowledge of God more than burnt offerings." (Hosea 6:6)

"The Lord is very compassionate and merciful [loving]." (James 5:14)

After Job suffered and was persecuted by Satan to test his faith, it was obvious that he became miserable and angered by the hardships he experienced. He lost all his precious goods on earth, his wife and children and also was afflicted by a terrible disease. God allowed Satan to attack him. God knew Job's faith in God was sincere and strong that he couldn't be tempted by Satan. When Job's friends told him, he must have committed a grievous sin that made him miserable. He insisted not so. Finally, he humbled himself when confronted by God, he was urged to stand up and to defend himself with wisdom and the will of God. God blessed him and restored his lost wealth. It was even doubled of what he previously had. He remarried and had three beautiful daughters and finally had a beautiful life. (Read also page 54, A Brief Story About Job)

In the book of Revelation, God preferred to use the word "forni- cation" for the word "idolatry," because He wants us to understand that those who can easily be deceived will know His feeling of love for them, being that God is a "jealous Gods" He would not want us to fall in Satan's camp. By loving Him, his beautiful plan for us is His eternal kingdom. We must show our love to Him through our obedi- ence to Him.

Since Moses' time, we were taught about the commandments of God. We were taught about loving God. He loved us first because He created us for His pleasure.

All His blessings are evidence of His love for us, His children. His laws are important. He teaches us how to love Him. Righteousness was emphasized in His teachings. He wants us to revere Him, not to fear, but to revere. This is because there is no fear in love, as righ- teousness acts are good works. He becomes our wall of protection. We improve as a result of obedience, and become better in life and be successful. We keep His commandments to be blessed. Disregard of His words will cause trouble, while we strive and struggle with endurance, He is always with us to help, for He says, "I shall never leave you, and shall never forsake you." (Hebrews 13:5)

While God is aware that men are easily swayed by his flesh, they do what they want to do, and neglect the words of God, as evilness in his heart continues, God has warned them that those who violate His laws will suffer consequences upon judgement time. We are judged by our works. The righteous will receive reward from God, while the unrighteous will have the punishment.

God sent His only begotten Son to the world that whosoever believes in Him will not perish, but will have everlasting life. When Jesus was on earth, He became the mediator of the old covenant by offering Himself to die on the cross. He fulfilled some of the written statutes, and ordinances through the sacrifice of His precious body and blood.

The sins of the world could not be justified without the use of sprinkling of blood of animals like bulls, goats, etc. by the priest to offer as in offering every year.

Jesus once and for all offered His precious blood as a sacrifice for us sinners to have salvation. From God's work, through His Son, His grace of repentance and forgiveness, we were brought nearer to God with a better promise for our salvation.

GOD'S TEACHINGS

"Do you not know that the unrighteous, will not inherit the Kingdom of God? Do not be deceived! Neither fornicators nor idolaters, nor adulterers, nor homosexuals, nor sodomites, nor thieves, nor covetous men, nor drunkards, nor revilers, nor extortionists will inherit the Kingdom of God" (1 Corinthians 6:9). Being in the flesh body, a person is weak and easily falls short of being righteous. We pray for strength and courage to build up a "renewed" person. When we repent sincerely, Christ will forgive us.

The flesh body is corrupt, easily deceived and sinful. It is stated in the bible that flesh and blood cannot enter the kingdom of God, unless it puts on incorruption or changed into a spiritual body. The flesh body dies, and it is sown to decay. It goes back to dust on earth, while the spirit will return to God, who gave life when you were born.

God is real. Look at all the things around you. With His great power to create the sky and the earth, with all things around it you can see that impossible things that cannot be made by man were made possible by God.

We must have faith to believe in His existence. Our mind is given to us to use wisdom and understanding. God wants us to know that He loves us. He sets His laws to be followed, for He wants us to be safe, healthy and strong, protected from the disgrace and wickedness of Satan.

"In Him, we have redemption in His blood, the forgiveness of sins, according to the richness of His grace." (Ephesians 1:7)

"All souls belong to Me." (Ezekiel 18:4)

He owns our souls and guides us, if you will allow Him.

He wants us to put on our gospel armor to protect us from Satan's method of operation, which consists of massive deceptions. If we follow God's advice, and follow His ways, our souls shall be rewarded for our righteous works in heaven.

What is our gospel armor? It says in Ephesians 6:13-17: "Therefore take up the whole armor of God, that you may be able to withstand in the evil day, and having done all, to stand. Stand therefore, having girded your waist with truth, having put on the breastplate of righteousness and having shod your feet with the preparation of the gospel of peace; above all, taking the shield of faith with which you will be able to quench all the fiery darts of the wicked one. And take the helmet of salvation, and the sword of the spirit, which is the Word of God."

> "Show me thy ways, O Lord; teach me thy paths. Lead me in thy truth
> and teach me: for Thou art the God of my salvation; on Thee do I want
> all the day." (Psalm 25:4-5)

His words are truth because God's words are eternal (I Peter 1:25). If you have time to read the Bible, in many places, you will find a wealth of promises He has made, that you can surely trust. Some are, as mentioned:

God gave you power over all your enemies in Christ's name. (Luke 10:19)

God's Spirit is the Holy Spirit. This is a positive force. Satan's spirit is the evil spirit, and this is a negative force. If we believe the power of God given to us to fight against the evil deed of Satan, it is based on truth and must be relied on.

"He who would love life and see good days, let him refrain his tongue from evil, and his lips from speaking guile; let him turn away from evil and do good; Let him seek peace and pursue it. For the eyes of the Lord are on the righteous, and His ears are open to their prayers; But the face of the Lord is against those who do evil." (1 Peter 3:10)

The greatest gift of God is love (1 Cor. 13:13).

With love, we keep God's commandments. It is a positive entity that we abide by hope, have faith and remain righteous. The Holy Spirit of God guides us to walk in peace.

You shall love your neighbor as yourself. All covetous acts are summed up in this saying: Not to harm by any means, your neighbor (Romans 13).

Love is the fulfillment of the law (Romans 13:10).

There is no law that violates a man's right. If love is a positive force that comes from God, we are honored, respected and blessed.

GOD'S BLESSINGS VS CURSES

Blessings

God blesses us with His love. Since the beginning of this earth age, we are led to a life with His protection and guidance to do His will. He gave His laws to be followed through Moses. The prophets of God were chosen to teach about His truth. With His Holy Spirit, He helps, guides, leads, and direct our lives to be righteous. It takes love to believe and hope in Him.

The true prophets of God are teaching His truth. People who have faith in Him, believe in His existence. His prophets in the likes of Abraham, Noah, Moses, David and others were found righteous and faithful that made them leaders of their generations. They showed their love of God, faith and hope in their works that brought their blessings. In spite of all hardships, problems and struggles, they were blessed. They endured to serve God and looked to the unforeseen future with hope that God's promises will be fulfilled. It says in the bible that they continued following God's commandments because they trusted in God's words to be fulfilled as they go on their journey like a pilgrim travelling toward their homeland as promised by God. These righteous elders presented us a cloud of testimony of hope, faith and love for God. They are all gone now and had not received the great promise, but it remains until Jesus Christ walks on earth as a better hope to all, to bring us to God at judgement time. Through Jesus Christ, we have a better covenant that is established; the grace of God through His son, brought repentance and forgiveness that whosoever love Him shall not perish but have everlasting life.

Curses

Curses are the opposite of blessings. It is a negative force that leads to punishment, decay, or death. Satan's other name is "Death", which is caused by confusion and deceptions of the world. God has a negative plan for those who live ungodly, they will be cast in the lake of fire. However, if we accept God's truth, God will also show His mercy and forgiveness.

This is in His time of anger, because of the people's disobedience and other sins committed against God.

Thus, says the Lord of hosts, "Behold, I will send on them the sword, the famine and the pestilence and will make them like rotten figs that cannot be eaten, they are so bad, and I will pursue them with the sword with famine and with pestilence, I will deliver them to trouble among all the kingdoms of the earth, to be a curse, an astonishment, a hissing and a reproach among all the nations where I have driven them." (Jeremiah 29:17-18)

SOME CURSES OR PUNISHMENT OF GOD (IN THE BEGINNING)

Due to wickedness, perversion, misconduct, and disobedience, the following divine judgments came upon the earth:

1. Noah's Flood—God commanded Noah to build an ark because He wanted to destroy all the land with a flood because of all of the evilness, behavior, and conduct of mankind, except Noah and his family. (See page about Noah's flood.)

2. The disappearance of Sodom and Gomorrah—God saw the widespread of wickedness of the people because of perversion, unbelief, and disobedience. He was very unhappy with the people being corrupt in the land (Genesis 19:24). Then the LORD brought upon them rain of brimstone and fire.

3. The plagues used by God against the Egyptian bondage led by Moses— Moses was used by God to save His children from the oppression of the Egyptians by means of plagues until the Israelites were finally set free to go to the Promised Land. "I will stretch out MY hand and strike Egypt with all MY wonders which I will do in it's midst; and after that, he will let you go" (Exodus 3:20).

The sins that will be committed by people on earth will also be avenged by God due to the violation of God's laws, disobedience, perversion, and immoral behaviors. Have a new heart by means of repentance and accepting His existence and loving God, then His blessings will be granted.

GOD'S LAWS

The Ten Commandments were given to Moses to be taught to the people so they would remember and follow them. In the Ten Commandments of God, there are two important things to consider: we must love God first with sincerity, in our minds, heart, and soul, and secondly, we must also love our families, brethren, and neighbors. That possibly would include all people around us on earth. If we must love people, we will not do any harm, such as lying, cheating, stealing, hurting, shaming, murdering, and coveting. All these laws of God are good and will keep us out of trouble and danger. This is the fulfillment of the law. We need to obey Him and follow His commandments because He loves us, His children.

Each one shall be judged according to his works (Revelation 20:13).

Example of righteous works:

1. The elect of God will be gathered to teach the unlearned of His truth,

2. Families serving each other,

3. Parents taking care of their children,

4. Children honoring and respecting their parents.

GOD'S JUDGMENT

God's judgment has two parts:

1. Punishment for our iniquities (sins committed). Sincere repentance is very important to be forgiven.

2. Reward (His blessings). We are rewarded as judged by our righteous acts. It is God's promise (Revelation 20:13).

However, God is a "cardio-knower." He can see in your spirit or mind, and He searches in your heart to see the sincerity and faith you have. In other words. He knows if you are lying or telling the truth (Romans 8:27).

1 Thessalonians 5:9

"God hath not appointed us to wrath, but to obtain salvation." 2 Peter 2:4

For if God did not spare the angels who sinned, but cast them down to hell and delivered them into chains of darkness, to be reserved for judgment; and did not spare the ancient world, but saved Noah, one of the eight people, a preacher of righteousness, bringing in the flood on the world of the ungodly; and turning the cities of Sodom and Gomorrah into ashes, condemned them to destruction, making them an example to those who afterward would live ungodly; and delivered righteous Lot, who was oppressed with the filthy conduct of the wicked.

GOD'S BLESSINGS AND PROMISES

With God's blessings, we become partakers of His Holiness. It takes a strong faith to follow His commandments. Without faith, we cannot please God. We please Him by being righteous. Abraham believed God, and God saw his faith was sincere, and when he offered his only son to God for a burnt offering. he promised

Abraham that he would be called the father of many nations and will multiply his descendants exceedingly. As time passed by, it came to a fulfillment that God's promise became a reality. The land of Caanan was the promised land that made the Israelites settle in at the wilderness. They were freed by the Egyptians from bondage through Moses. That generation continues to spread out God's blessings even to these times and became many nations of the Middle East.

We can say that the blessings of God flows continuously because of faith. God's covenant with His love, continues as it states in the bible (John 3:16) "God sent His one and only begotten Son to earth that whosoever believe in Him shall not perish but have everlasting life". This is why the second covenant became a better promise for us (refer to p. 35-36) for the first covenant thru Moses' laws, then thru the crucifixion of Jesus Christ. He made it through the grace of Jesus Christ that with repentance and forgiveness, we are being brought closer to God. When Jesus Christ walked on earth among us, He did His ministerial works preaching God's words, healing the sick, giving sight to the blind, making the lame walk, and healing evil torments. He was hated for His many righteous acts by many unbelievers until He was crucified by the Roman soldiers and the Kenites. He made a lot of sacrifices for the sake of the sinners he offered Himself to die on the cross to be able to take part in our salvation by defeating death who is Satan.

GOD'S WARNINGS

The wrath of God is appointed at the end times because the enemy will be deception and confusion. Calamities and different kinds of natural disasters and adversities, such as earthquakes, famine, pestilences, and diseases, will happen because of idolatry, false teachings, and wickedness. These acts of God have already been prophesied, so we must be prepared. Jesus is coming to earth, not as a babe to be crucified in His adult life and resurrected, but to hold a rod of iron and a sword to strike the nations to rule as a Lord of lords and King of kings.

> *"Behold, the days are coming says the Lord God, that I will send a famine on the land, not a famine of bread, nor a thirst for water, but of hearing the words of the Lord.*
>
> *They shall wander from sea to sea, and from north to east, they shall run to and fro, seeking the word of the Lord, but shall not find it."* (Amos 8:11-12)

The book of Amos tells about the fury of God because of many transgressions. It will be just like in the evil times when God will pour out His vial of wrath on earth as prophesied. The sins are due to disregard of God's laws, unrighteousness, perversions, injustices, idolatry, and disobedience. Due to the evilness of the times, God will release His punishment of calamities, destruction of things, darkness in the land, including sending the "locust army" to devour the green trees and plants. We must therefore humble ourselves and have a change of heart to a newness of righteousness as He says, "Return to Me." Repent sincerely and be forgiven. "Seek Me and live. Seek good and not evil that you may live: so, the Lord God of hosts will be with you." Hate evil, love good: establish justice in the gate "But let justice run down like water, and righteousness like a mighty stream." (Amos 5:24).

Amos is one of God's prophets who holds the secret of God by His mystery. He revealed that Satan's coming to earth will be as lightning that strikes when he appears to sit in God's temple in Jerusalem to play the role of Jesus to be worshipped (Luke 10:8).

It is of great importance that people's attention must be awakened to the truth of God to prepare for the hard times (worst events) that are coming, for God's words of wrath and vengeance will be poured out on the unlearned, ignorant, disobedient of His words, and those deceived by our spiritual enemies. Our enemy is the wicked one (Satan) and his supporters, like the Kenites' (Cain's offspring), evil angels, demons, and false prophets.

I pray and hope that God's message will be absorbed in our minds to prepare us for safety and hope for God's salvation. Therefore, repentance and forgiveness are given if we ask God for them.

The Parables

Jesus spoke:

> *"I will open my mouth in parables. I will utter things which has been kept secret from the foundation of the world." (Matthew 13:35)*

Jesus reveals the hidden secrets of God, which are the parables. For those who know about the words of God, they are expected to understand and will be given more knowledge, but to those who are ignorant, whatever they know will be taken away from them. For our awareness of the truth, we have eyes to see, and we have ears to hear, and understand the words of God.

> *"Behold, I tell you a mystery. We shall not all sleep, but we shall all be changed in a moment in the twinkling of an eye, at the last trumpet. For the trumpet will sound, and the dead will be raised incorruptible and we shall all be changed." (1 Corinthians 15:51)*

At the sound of the last trumpet of God, Jesus, the Son of God, will appear. All and everything will be changed into spirit. This is the millennium when we will all see Him and "every knee" will bow to Him, and He will see our fate. At the end of the millennium, we shall all be present at the white throne judgment of the highest court of our Father.

Jesus Speaking about the Parable of the Tares:

> *Another parable He put forth to them, saying: "The kingdom of heaven is like a man who sowed good seed in his field; but while men slept, his enemy came and sowed tares among the wheat and went his way. But when the grain had sprouted and produced a crop, then the tares also appeared. So the servants of the owner came and said to him, 'Sir, did you not sow good seed in your field? How then does it have tares?' He said to them, 'An enemy has done this.' The servants said to him, 'Do you want us then to go and gather them up?' But he said, 'No, lest while you gather up the tares you also uproot the wheat with them. Let both grow together until the harvest, and at the time of harvest I will say to the reapers, "First gather together the tares and bind them in bundles to burn them, but gather the wheat into my barn." '"*

All these things Jesus spoke to the multitude in parables; and without a parable He did not speak to them, 35 that it might be fulfilled which was spoken by the prophet, saying:

"I will open My mouth in parables;

I will utter things kept secret from the foundation of the world."

Then Jesus sent the multitude away and went into the house. And His disciples came to Him, saying, "Explain to us the parable of the tares of the field."

He answered and said to them: "He who sows the good seed is the Son of Man. The field is the world, the good seeds are the sons of the kingdom, but the tares are the sons of the wicked one. The enemy who sowed them is the devil, the harvest is the end of the age, and the reapers are the angels. Therefore as the tares are gathered and burned in the fire, so it will be at the end of that age.

(Matthew 13:24-30, 34-40)

The knowledge we have about the Word of God will make us aware of the events of calamities or plagues that will come at the end of the times. We must wait for Jesus Christ and remain calm, bold, and wise. We must be careful not to be deceived with teachings of the traditions of man. Grow with good discipline to be more useful to God.

THE PARABLE OF THE FIG TREE

"Beware of false prophets who come to you in ravenous clothing, but inwardly they are ravenous wolves. You will know them by their fruit" (Matthew 7:15-16).

All prophecies made will be fulfilled until Christ appears at the millennium. The teachers must preach the truth of God instead of the traditions of man. Some preachers take advantage of ignorant people even to the extent of "begging" for money in return for their false teachings. At the final generation (end times), when our Lord Jesus Christ comes, no one knows the time or hour. That is why He insists that we learn the parable of the fig tree to know the chronological order of events that will take place so that we can prepare ourselves and be guided in what to do. We must be strong in our faith and keep the seal in our minds about God's truth to avoid deception. We are told to watch!

The parable of the fig tree has three generations involved:

1. 40 generations—Before Christ walked on the earth, the children of God (the Hebrews) wandered in the wilderness before they entered the Promised Land.

2. 70 generations—After Christ walked on earth, Israel and Judah first separated, but then returned and became a nation. This occurred in 1948.

3. 120 generations—This year is from 1948, in which the fig tree was planted as a shoot and is continuously growing until Jesus Christ returns to earth.

We are all waiting for the return of Jesus Christ. No one knows the time. So, He says, "Watch and pray that we must know the seasons," as He said (Matthew 24:34-35) "Assuredly, I say to you, this generation will by no means pass away until all these things [prophecies] are fulfilled." Watch therefore you also be ready, for the Son of Man is coming at an hour when you do not expect Him." You are not expecting Him, because you already have accepted the false Jesus, whom you thought was the true Christ. Don't be deceived!

PREACHING

Go into all the world and preach the gospel to all the creations (Mark 16:15).

Be ready in season and out of season. Convince, rebuke, exhort with long suffering and teaching. (2 Timothy 4:2) And this gospel of the kingdom will be preached in all the world as a witness to all the nations and then the end will come. (Matthew 24:14)

He gave Moses the law, the Ten Commandments of God to be taught, remembered, and followed. Jesus, the only begotten Son of God, taught His disciples by speaking in parables. They taught the gentiles about God, His mystery, which has been kept secret and now has been revealed to His saints (Amos 3:7).

The preaching of God's prophets to the people in all wisdom is to present every man perfect in Jesus Christ.

God teaches us to put our gospel armor on to protect us from Satan's method of operation, which consists of massive deceptions. If we follow God's advices, we shall be rewarded for our works at judgment time.

Go your way, behold I sent you out as lambs among wolves. (Luke 10:3)

Jesus knew that many people were victims of Satan in different cities. He saw that the "harvest" of many deceived people was more than the undeceived. So, he added seventy preachers more besides his disciples to teach and heal those afflicted with illnesses and victims of evil torment. When they came back to Jesus, they reported with gladness that the evil spirits were afraid of their words using Jesus Christ's name, and they obeyed.

> *And He said to them, "I saw Satan fall like lightning from heaven. Behold, I give you the authority to trample on serpents and scorpions, and over all the power of the enemy, and nothing shall by any means hurt you. Nevertheless do not rejoice in this, that the spirits are subject to you, but rather rejoice because your names are written in heaven." (Luke 10:18-20)*

His disciples and teachers that He sent out were sealed with the knowledge of God (in their minds), and therefore, they knew how to handle deceptions of the wicked enemies.

When we wake up to the truth of God, the gospel must be spread as God approves it to preach His words. It is necessary to teach our families, friends, and neighbors for the sake of love and righteousness. We would like for them to be included in God's salvation, and to prevent them from the damnation or chaotic events that cause corruption of the world, which leads to God's wrath at the end times.

> *And Jesus went about all the cities' villages, in their synagogue, preaching the gospel of the Kingdom and healing every sickness and every disease among the people. (Matthew 9:35)*

There was a time when Jesus taught at the synagogue and happened to read from the book of Isaiah 61:1-3. Luke 4:18:

> *"The Spirit of the Lord God is upon Me, Because the Lord has anointed Me To preach good tidings to the poor; He has sent Me to heal the brokenhearted, To proclaim liberty to the captives, And the opening of the prison to those who are bound; To proclaim the acceptable year of the Lord, And the day of vengeance of our God; To comfort all who mourn, To console those who mourn in Zion, To give them beauty for ashes, The oil of joy for mourning, The garment of praise for the spirit of heaviness;*
>
> *That they may be called trees of righteousness, The planting of the Lord, that He may be glorified."*

He stopped reading and closed the book and said, "Today this scripture is fulfilled in your hearing." He was telling the people what the Son of God, who was anointed, was doing as a preacher to let them know the truth about God's salvation and God's vengeance and wrath to happen at the end times, which is yet to happen.

God is the hope and glory of His people. They marveled at Jesus' teaching of wisdom at His very young age. He answered questions of Bible scholars with much authority.

THE BIBLE

The Bible is the way to the truth.

God loves all His children. This is why His love letter (Bible) is written for us to know and understand the coming events that are unfolding and be warned of the bitter and painful effects of great calamities and disasters that are coming as a result of God's wrath because of ignorance and disobedience of His words.

It is a very important book that God had written through his prophets that contains His words. It consists of man, and events of the past, as well as present and future occurrences as prophesied until the end of the age. Our Father in heaven, who created all things, sends us His message of love and warns us about the coming of the anti-Christ, who will deceive the world and will bring confusion and trouble. There will be serious consequences for disobedience and punishments meted out due to violations of Gods' laws. The Bible contains the precious teachings of God that will keep us safe, out of trouble, keep us healthy, happy, and successful in life. We need to absorb the precious teachings of God in our minds so that we are not deceived by Satan and the anti-Christ.

> *For thus sayeth the Lord, that created the heavens, God Himself that formed and made it; He had established it, He created it not in vain, He found it to be inhabited: "I am the Lord, and there is no other".*
> *(Isaiah 45:18)*

The words of God are all about His omnipotence, with all His creations, His love for us, and His only begotten Son Jesus Christ.

The words of God are real, therefore, as followers of our Father, and Jesus Christ, we must accept and show our love by obedience for righteousness, and avoid or eliminate the lies and falsehood of Satan, which are the traditions of man that are causing deceptions and confusions, especially at the end of the age.

He expresses His love and message of truth to His children through His prophet to be read by all.

> *"I do not want your burnt offerings. I desire mercy (love) and the knowledge of God more than anything". (Hosea 6:6)*

He wants us to love Him. He deserves to be loved because He is our Creator who made everything on earth for His pleasure, all about Him, His wonderful creations, His teachings, and His beautiful plan for us, and His warnings about the dangers and calamities and plagues that are coming at the end times. All are written to be learned, and therefore the goal of salvation is achieved. If we obey God's words, we can be

confident that His blessings are with us. He warns us to be alert, and by reading, we must understand His words of truth to be able to handle and prepare ourselves from the attacks of our enemies (Satan and his army) with their lies and deceptions, which will easily lead us to confusion and commit sin. He is happy if we obey Him and be righteous, for our salvation is through His Son Jesus Christ. This is how we are blessed with His precious gift which is eternal life!

Usually, when people read the book of Revelation, with less education and lack of knowledge, they become upset and fail to understand its message. Some think negatively that God will destroy the earth. No! Not at all. The new heaven and new earth will be astonishingly beautiful and comfortable, which will be established by God here on earth in Jerusalem. This is His favorite place in all the universe. He loves us. He also expects us to follow Him. He has a wonderful plan for us, whom He loves. That is why He wrote the Bible to let us have His message to read and be guided and saved from catastrophes and chaos that are to come upon the world. His main message: be careful and be wise, do not be deceived, for Satan is coming with his massive lies and deceptions to mislead people.

Satan is coming peacefully and prosperously (Daniel 11:21-24). The opposite of war is peace. When there is rumor of peace, peace, peace, be warned! That is the season when Satan and the anti-Christ will come to play the role of the false Messiah. Don't be troubled, because if you are standing firm on the Rock (Jesus) and have the seal of knowledge of God, you are protected!

THE HOLY SPIRIT OF GOD

In the Hebrew language, "ruach" means an invisible "force." Life is our spirit that comes from God and that returns to God upon death.

These are seven manifestations or characters of the Holy Spirit of God (Revelation 5:12):

Power, Riches, Wisdom, Strength, Honor, Glory, Blessings.

The Spirit of God is the Holy Spirit, who is the third person of the Trinity with His Divine manifestation in the creation of all things created through His Divine power:

1. In creation giving life and death—The Spirit is responsible in giving life, also death.

2. Blessings to people—Divine favors, kindness, and grace given by God.

3. Judgments according to works—Upon corrections and punishments and reward for good deeds.

The Holy Spirit is a positive entity who is present on earth. God puts our souls in the womb when we are conceived to have life and puts us off to death in the flesh and brings us alive in the spirit for judgment.

> *"But the fruit of the spirit is love, peace, joy, patience, kindness, godliness, faithfulness, gentleness, self-control, against such things there is no law". (Galatians 5:22)*

The Spirit of Jehovah (Yahoveh) is Jehovah Himself (Our heavenly Father) in His manifestation of Invisible Divine Power.

A. The Invisible Divine Power of God manifesting in:

1. Creation—"And the Spirit of God was hovering over the face of the waters" (Genesis 1:2).

2. In giving life—"I put my 'Spirit' in you, and you shall live" (Ezekiel 37:14).

3. In executing judgment—"And with the blast of Your nostrils, the waters were gathered together" (Exodus 15:8).

4. Words used

    a. Blast (2 Samuel 22:16); Then the channels of the sea were seen, The foundations of the world were uncovered, At the rebuke of the Lord, At the blast of the breath of His nostrils.

    b.   Breath (Job 4:9); By the blast of God they perish, And by the breath of His anger they are consumed.

    c.   Spirit (Isaiah 4:4); When the Lord has washed away the filth of the daughters of Zion, and purged the blood of Jerusalem from her midst, by the spirit of judgment and by the spirit of burning,

The Holy Spirit is present as a positive force, just as Satan's spirit is also around, which is the negative spirit.

B.   The "Invisible" Part of Man: Psychological—giving life at birth and returning to God at the death of the flesh.

C.   The "Invisible" Characteristics of Man—manifesting themselves in state of mind and feeling. References of each character or words are given below:

    1.   Mind (Genesis 26:35); "And they were a grief of mind to Isaac and Rebekah."

    2.   Breath (Job 19:17); "My breath is offensive to my wife, And I am repulsive to the children of my own body."

    3.   Courage (Joshua 2:11); "And as soon as we heard *these things*, our hearts melted; neither did there remain any more courage in anyone because of you, for the Lord your God, He is God in heaven above and on earth beneath."

    4.   Anger (Judges 8:3); "God has delivered into your hands the princes of Midian, Oreb and Zeeb. And what was I able to do in comparison with you?" Then their anger toward him subsided when he said that."

    5.   Blast (Isaiah 25:4); "For You have been a strength to the poor, A strength to the needy in his distress, A refuge from the storm, A shade from the heat; For the blast of the terrible ones is as a storm against the wall."

    6.   Spirit (Numbers 5:14); "if the spirit of jealousy comes upon him and he becomes jealous of his wife, who has defiled herself; or if the spirit of jealousy comes upon him and he becomes jealous of his wife, although she has not defiled herself"

D.   The "Invisible" spirit beings:

    1.   Angels (Psalm 104:4); "Who makes His angels spirits, His ministers a flame of fire."

    2.   Cherubim (Ezekiel 10:17); "When *the cherubim* stood still, the *wheels* stood still, and when one was lifted up, the other lifted itself up, for the spirit of the living creature was in them."

    3.   Neutral spirits (undetermined) (Job 4:15): "Then a spirit passed before my face; The hair on my body stood up."

4. Evil angels (distressing spirits) (1 Samuel 16:14); "But the Spirit of the Lord departed from Saul, and a distressing spirit from the Lord troubled him."

E. The "Invisible" manifestation of atmosphere:

1. Wind or winds (Numbers 11:31); "Now a wind went out from the Lord, and it brought quail from the sea and left them fluttering near the camp, about a day's journey on this side and about a day's journey on the other side, all around the camp, and about two cubits above the surface of the ground."

2. Whirlwind (Ezekiel 1:4); "Then I looked, and behold, a whirlwind was coming out of the north, a great cloud with raging fire engulfing itself; and brightness was all around it and radiating out of its midst like the color of amber, out of the midst of the fire."

3. Windy (Psalm 55:8) "I would hasten my escape From the windy storm and tempest."

4. Spirits (Zachariah 6:5) "And the angel answered and said to me, "These are four spirits of heaven, who go out from their station before the Lord of all the earth."

5. Air (Job 41:16); "One is so near another That no air can come between them;"

6. Tempest (Psalm 11:6): "Upon the wicked, he shall rain snares, fire and brimstone, and an horrible tempest: this shall be the portion of their cup.

7. Blast (Exodus 15:8); "And with the blast of Your nostrils The waters were gathered together; The floods stood upright like a heap; The depths congealed in the heart of the sea."

8. Quarters (of the four winds) (1 Chronicles 9:24); "The gatekeepers were assigned to the four directions: the east, west, north, and south."

9. Side or sides (of the four winds) (Jeremiah 52:23); "There were ninety-six pomegranates on the sides; all the pomegranates, all around on the network, were one hundred."

Some examples used to represent the power of the Holy Spirit:

1. Wind or winds (Matthew 24:31); "And He will send His angels with a great sound of a trumpet, and they will gather together His elect from the four winds, from one end of heaven to the other."

2. Whirlwind (Job 38:1); "Then the Lord answered Job out of the whirlwind, and said:

"Who is this who darkens counsel

By words without knowledge?

3.   Dove (The spirit that touched Jesus' baptism) (Matthew 3:16); "When He had been baptized, Jesus came up immediately from the water; and behold, the heavens were opened to Him, and He saw the Spirit of God descending like a dove and alighting upon Him."

4.   Rainbow (The bow of heaven seen after the flood of Noah) (Revelation 4:3); "And He who sat there was[a] like a jasper and a sardius stone in appearance; and there was a rainbow around the throne, in appearance like an emerald."

5.   Fire (from the bush when Moses saw a burning bush that was not consumed) (Exodus 3:2); "And the Angel of the Lord appeared to him in a flame of fire from the midst of a bush. So he looked, and behold, the bush was burning with fire, but the bush was not consumed."

Living or Walking in the Holy Spirit

Author's Note:

Remember our bodies are made up of two kinds: one is the flesh body the second is the spiritual body.

We are being taught by God that we must live and walk in the Spirit, not by the flesh, because the works of the flesh are sinful.

> *"But the fruits of the Holy Spirit are: love, peace, joy, long suffering (patience), kindness, goodness, faithfulness, gentleness, and self-control". (Galatians 5:22)*

When Jesus Christ was crucified, He nailed the sins of the world to the cross and the old practice of circumcision of flesh, which is bloodletting, and is no longer practiced. Instead, nowadays it is the circumcision of the heart, which means living in the spirit, which is true faith in Jesus Christ with love.

JESUS CHRIST

Prophecy found in Isaiah 7:14: "Behold the virgin shall conceive and bear a Son and shall call Him Emmanuel (God with us)

Other Names:

1. The Image of the Invisible God—Colossians 1:15: He is the image of the invisible God, the firstborn over all creations

2. The Messiah—John 4:25: The woman said to Him, I know that Messiah is "coming" (Who is called Christ). "When He comes, He will tell us all things." Jesus said to her, "I who speak to you am He."

3. The WORD—John 1:14: In the beginning was the WORD, and the WORD was with God, and the WORD was God.

4. Lamb of God—John 4:36: And looking at Jesus as He walked, He said, "Behold the Lamb of God."

5. The Morning Star—Revelation 22:16: "I Jesus, I have sent My angel to testify to you these things in the churches. I am the root and the offspring of David, the Bright and Morning Star."

6. The Root of David (Revelation 5:5); "But one of the elders said to me, "Do not weep. Behold, the Lion of the tribe of Judah, the Root of David, has prevailed to open the scroll and to loose[a] its seven seals."

7. The Living Water—John 1:35: And Jesus said to them, "I Am the Bread of Life. He who comes to Me shall never hunger and he who believes in Me shall never thirst."

8. The Living Bread—(John 6:51); "I am the living bread which came down from heaven. If anyone eats of this bread, he will live forever; and the bread that I shall give is My flesh, which I shall give for the life of the world."

9. Our Passover—He is the Highest Holiday of Christians. I Corinthian 5:7 Therefore, purge out the old leaven that you may be a new lamp, since you truly are unleavened, for indeed, Christ, our Passover, was sacrificed for us.

10. Son of God—John 1:34 I have seen and testified that this is the Son of God.

11. The Rock—1 Corinthian 10:4: And all drank the same spiritual drink. For they drank of that spiritual Rock that followed them, and that Rock was Christ.

12. Lord of lords, King of kings—Revelation 19:16: And He has on His robe and His thigh, a name written: King of kings and Lord of lords. He is worthy to be called as such because He is going to rule all the nations of the world with a rod of iron to discipline, correct and give total peace in His new kingdom of the Almighty God in Jerusalem.

13. The Way, the Truth, and the Life (John 14:6) "I am the Way, the Truth, and the Life. No one comes to the Father except through Me."

JESUS, WITH HIS PARENTS IN THE FLESH, MARY AND JOSEPH

Mary, a virgin betrothed to a man named Joseph of the house of David, had found favor with God. "You will conceive in your womb and bring forth a Son and shall call His name Jesus. He will be great and will be called Son of the Highest," and the Lord God will give Him the throne of His father David" (Luke 1:30).

The angel answered to Mary, "The Holy Spirit will come upon you, and the power of the Highest will overshadow you; therefore, also that Holy One who is to be born will be called the Son of God."

So, Joseph, the adopted father of Jesus, and Mary, His mother, raised him, and every year they all attended the feast of Passover in Jerusalem (Luke 1:3-5).

HIS COMING TO EARTH

His coming to earth began on the period of His conception, which is December 25th. (Nativity date—September 29, 4 BC)[*1]

The announcement of Mary's pregnancy with Jesus was first told to Elizabeth, her cousin, who was pregnant with John the Baptist, when Mary visited her at the hill country of Judah. Upon her greetings, and with excitement, the child in Elizabeth's womb leaped for joy, and she was filled with the Holy Spirit. He, Jesus was born on September 29, 4 BC. It is all right to celebrate Christmas on December 25, since Jesus Christ has appeared in the flesh first in the world. That day was the day of Jesus Christ's conception. The Holy Spirit was present. For further reference, read well with understanding the book of Luke in the Bible.

Upon conception, God places a soul in the womb. It came to pass that Jesus, the boy grew and became strong in Spirit, filled with wisdom, and the grace of God was upon Him (Luke 1:40).

He started His life in a very humble way. He was born as a babe laid in a manger and lived His boyhood as a son of a carpenter with His adopted father, Joseph. He taught as a teacher of His disciples and was crucified, died, and was resurrected to heaven after three days.

---

*   Ref. Companion Bible: Nativity date No. 179 page 197

His parents went to Jerusalem every year, at the feast of the Passover. When he was twelve years old, he was found at the synagogue talking and listening to teachers, and all who heard him were astonished at his understanding and answers. It should not be a surprise for us because Jesus Christ is the Living Word.

In the beginning was the Word, and the Word was with God, and the Word was God (John 1).

And they were astonished at His teaching, for His word was with authority. (Luke 4:32)

His cousin was John the Baptist, a Levitical priest, son of Zacharias and Elizabeth, who are both full blooded Levitical priests. John was preaching a baptism of repentance for the remission of sins. He was a preacher in the region of Jordan.

His Ministry on Earth

Jesus began His ministry at the age of about thirty years old. He was led by the Holy Spirit to the wilderness and was tempted by the devil for forty days. He ate nothing and was hungry but overcame His suffering.

The devil tempted Him: "If you are the Son of God, command that these stones become bread." But He answered and said, "It is written, man shall not live by bread alone, but by every word that proceeds from the mouth of God." Then the devil took Him up into the Holy city, set Him into the pinnacle of the temple, and said to Him, "If you are the Son of God, throw yourself down. For it is written: He (God) shall give His angels charge concerning You, and it is in their hands, they shall bear You up lest, you dash Your foot against a stone." Jesus said to him, it is written again, "You shall not tempt the Lord your God." Again, the devil took Him up on an exceedingly high mountain and showed Him all the kingdom of the world and their glory. And he said to Him, "All these things I will give You if You will fall down and worship me." And then Jesus said to him, Then Jesus said to him, "Away with you Satan! For it is written you shall worship Lord your God, and Him only you shall serve." Then, the devil left Him (Matthew 4)-11).

He was preaching and teaching the people about the Word of God. He healed many people with different kinds of illnesses, gave sight to the blind, and delivered those who were tormented by evil or uncleaned spirits. He even raised some who were dead. He chose His twelve apostles (teacher) from His disciples (students). Many believed in Him; however, there were also those who did not agree with Him. Because of jealousy and hatred, the Kenites secretly planned to kill Him, which led to his crucifixion, because they were the ones who insisted and shouted, "Crucify Him! Crucify Him!" when He was presented to Pilate for trial (Mark 15:13).

CRUCIFIXION OF JESUS CHRIST

He was crucified with the transgressors. He bore sins of many and made intercessory for the transgressors. (Isaiah 53:12)

With Him, they also crucified two robbers, one on His right and the other on the left. So, the Scriptures were fulfilled, which say, "And He was numbered with the transgressors" (Mark 15:28).

Judas, one of Jesus' disciples, betrayed Him and was given thirty pieces of silver by the chief priest and elders of the church to deliver Jesus to the chief priest. The chief priest, scribes, and elders of the people had planned to kill Jesus. They hated Jesus for no reason but could not harm Him, as they were afraid of a possible riot from the crowd of sinners. Then one of the twelve disciples, named Judas Iscariot, went to the chief priests and delivered Jesus to them for thirty pieces of silver. Then Judas, His betrayer, seeing that he had been condemned, became remorseful and brought back thirty pieces of silver to the chief priests and elders, saying, *"I have sinned by betraying innocent blood."* Then, he threw down the pieces of silver in the temple and went out and hanged himself (Matthew 27:5).

The last written statement above is in contrary with what is written below:

Now, this man purchased a field with the wages of inequity, and falling head long, he burst open in the middle and all his entrails gushed out. (Acts 1:18)

He could not have committed suicide but must have had someone help him hang himself because his midsection burst open and his entrails gushed out.

This must have been done by the Kenites, in the same manner that they did to Christ, who was set out to die on the cross. Judas repented because he was remorseful (repented) of what they did to Jesus, but remember, God will be the judge.

The veil of the temple was torn into two from top to bottom. There were earthquakes, and the rocks were split. (Matthew 27:51)

During Jesus' crucifixion at the temple, the high priest was prevented from coming into the Holy of Holies, where Jesus was in that moment. Anyone was free to enter without the aid of a priest because God always encourages us to come to Him to repent to be forgiven of our sins. It was a miracle! The curtain was ripped wide open in that room, which was meant that anyone was invited to come in. We must hear Him talk to us.

Christ suffered once for sinners that he might bring us to God being put to death in the flesh but made alive by the Spirit. He went and preached to the spirits in prison [paradise]. (1 Peter 3:19)

When Jesus Christ was in the tomb, His spirit went to paradise to preach to all who have died, all the way to the beginning to offer His grace of repentance and forgiveness and was able to be accepted by many as the law of God through Moses became a better promise during Jesus Christ's time. Those people who have died and were under the law of the ten commandments were given a chance under Christ's repentance and forgiveness mainly for salvation to justify sin.

Jesus was crucified to defeat death (Hebrew 2:14)

JESUS' RESURRECTION

He died at 3 p.m., Wednesday, and was laid in the tomb on that evening. Hebrew time to consider is from sunset to sunset.

> *"Now when He rose early in the first day of the week, He appeared first to Mary Magdalene, out of whom He had cast out seven demons. She went and told those who had been with Him, as they mourned and wept." (Mark 16:9-10)*

"And when they heard that He was alive and had been seen by her, they did not believe. After that, He appeared in another form to two of them as they walked and went into the country. And they went and told it to the rest, but they did not believe them either." (Mark 16:11-13)

Later He appeared to the eleven as they sat at the table; and He rebuked their unbelief and hardness of heart, because they did not believe those who had seen Him after He had risen. And He said to them, "Go into all the world and preach the gospel to every creature" (Mark 16:14).

"He who believes and is baptized will be saved; but he who does not believe will be condemned.

And these signs will follow those who believe: In My name they will cast out demons; they will speak with new tongues; they will take up serpents; and if they drink anything deadly, it will be by no means hurt them; they will lay hands on the sick, and they will recover" (Mark 16:18). This means that you will know how to handle the evil spirit because you have God's truth.

"So then, after the Lord had spoken to them, He was received up into heaven and sat down at the right hand of God" (Mark 16:19).

JESUS' TEACHINGS

I saw Satan fall like lighting from heaven, "Behold I give you the authority to trample on serpents and scorpions and over all the power of the enemy [Satan] and nothing shall by any means hurt you" (Luke 10:18).

The true believers with strong faith who have the seal of God in their minds would know how to handle deceptions by the wicked ones.

PRAYERS

How do we pray? A prayer is a form of talking to God. With prayer, you praise the Lord for His wonderful ways and blessings. Humble yourself to ask for your wishes and requests to be blessed according to His will. Always thank God for everything He blesses you with.

We would always ask in prayer according to His will, and He hears us while we know that we have our petitions that we have asked of Him (Matthew 21:22).

God hears the prayers of the righteous. His leadership and guidance are very important to our lives. He says to us "Be holy," "Be blameless," and we are blessed.

God always is a very loving and merciful God. He likes for us to welcome Him into our lives and to love Him. He created us for His pleasure. He wants us to talk to Him, so He can open and "justify" us and give us His blessings. In fact, He wants us to repent of our sins to be forgiven and be happy to have eternal life. We must not forget to pray in our daily life. We need peace and His guidance and directions to whatever problems we may encounter during our busy day.

Whatever things you ask, when you pray, believe that you received them, and you will have them (Mark 11:24).

God is Spirit. And those who worship Him must worship Him in Spirit and truth (John 4:24).

I say to you that if two of you agree on earth concerning anything that they ask, it will be done for him by my Father in heaven (Matthew 18:19-20).

Enter into His gates with thanksgiving and into His courts with praise. Be thankful to Him and bless His name. For the Lord is good; His mercy is everlasting, and His truth endures through all generations (Psalm 100:4).

We worship not only on special days or weekends, but we pray every day, for we find rest (Sabbath day) with Jesus, with whom we have peace of mind. Jesus Christ is Lord of our Sabbath (Luke 6:5).

When you pray, do not use vain repetitions as the heathen do. For they think that they will be heard for their many words. We must always find time to commune with our God, the Father. In thesemodern days of our world, families are extremely busy with lots of daily tasks and responsibilities. A safe and convenient way to worship God is at home. If we choose to watch religious programs, we must make sure the preacher teaches the truth of God, such as the Shepherd's Chapel, where they teach the Bible chapter by chapter and verse by verse to explain God's words and not to lose track of His message, or we can choose to study the Bible privately or individually to get access to the true words of God.

It is important to communicate with our Almighty God, because spiritually speaking, we need to feed our souls, not only physical food for the flesh body. We are not sure that church outside our home is the true church that teaches the true gospel. We would not want towaste our time and be misled from the truth: we find blessing with our prayers. God's message of love is expressed in many ways: through His words in the book of Psalms and Proverbs, which give knowledge about His wonders and advices, through His health laws, in the book of Deuteronomy and Leviticus, to know what foods are safe and healthy to eat, and to avoid trouble and be successful. For those people who ignore God's words, they tend to cause folly and become sinners. We are warned of the consequences that will happen as laid by God in seasons.

> *"Be afraid of the Sword for yourselves, for wrath brings the punishment of the sword that you may know there is a judgement". (Job 19:29)*

The "Sword" means Jesus' tongue that has two sharp sides to cut falsehoods and bring the truth. (Rev 1:16, 19:15)

JESUS' AUTHORITY

"All authorities had been given to Me in heaven and on earth". (Matthew 28:18).

God gave you power over all your enemies in Christ's name. In whatever negative situation you are involved, you should use the name of Jesus Christ in prayers. It will bring relief, whether to eliminate evil spirits or evil torments for healing. Always pray in the name of Jesus Christ (Luke 10:19).

"Is anyone among you sick? Let him call on the elders of the church, and let them pray over him, anointing him with blessed oil in the name of the Lord Jesus Christ." And the Lord will bring him up and if he has committed sin, he will be forgiven (James 5:14).

HEALING

If a person is troubled with sickness or any kind of affliction that causes physical or mental distress, we must anoint with the blessed oil, ask God with prayers for healing will uplift our spirit.

Jesus healed multitudes of people while preaching. A woman, with a flow of blood for twelve years, believed in faith that if she could only touch His garment she would get well. Jesus felt her touching His clothes while among the crowd and said: *"Be of good cheer, daughter, your faith has made you well"* (Matthew 9:35).

The use of olive oil for anointing illnesses received healings, including those tormented by evil spirits were freed by prayers using the name of Jesus Christ.

But when the multitudes know it, they followed Him, and He received them and spoke to them about the kingdom of God and healed those who need healing. (Matthew 9:11)

And certain women who had been healed of evil spirits and infirmities. Mary Magdalene out of whom had come seven demons. (Luke 8:2)

Then He healed many who were sick with various diseases and cast out many demons to speak because they knew Him. (Mark 1:34)

Then the blind and the lame came to Him in the temple and He healed them. (Matthew 21:14)

But He was wounded for our transgressions, He was bruised for our iniquities; the chastisement of our peace was upon Him, and with His stripes we are healed. (Isaiah 53:5)

Baptism

Jesus was the only one perfect in the flesh; however, He allowed John the Baptist, His cousin, to baptize Him, to show us an example of righteousness. "Repent and be baptized. Believe that Jesus Christ died on the cross and resurrected in the name of the Father, Son, and the Holy Spirit," and you are forgiven. Many people ask: at what age are we supposed to be baptized? When a person is able to know] the difference between right and wrong is the best time. The age of naccountability is not specifically known. It varies. It can be from age six to sixty. It depends on how a person thinks (or according to the maturity of the mind). With baptism, repentance and forgiveness are a form of cleansing out the soul.

> *"John came baptizing in the wilderness and preaching a baptism for the remission of sins." (Mark 1:4)*
>
> *After Jesus was risen, the eleven disciples worshipped Him, but some doubted. He said, "all authority has been given to Me in heaven and on earth. Go therefore and make disciples of all the nations baptizing them in the name of the Father, the Son, and the Holy Spirit, teaching them to observe all things that I have commanded you, and lo, I am with you always, even to the end of the age" (Matthew 28:18)*
>
> *"He who believes and is baptized will be saved. But he who does not believe will be condemned." (Mark 16:16)*

We are baptized by submerging our body into the water believing that Christ died and while He was in the tomb and in the working of God, He also was raised from the dead. In the likeness of Christ's death, when we are baptized, we are buried with Him and also shall be raised in the likeness of His resurrection. We pray to cleanse our sins, for with Christ's grace, we repent and are forgiven.

MYSTERY

Sometimes we are unmindful of the things that are true because we don't understand, and we choose to neglect to know or discover the truth.

> *The mystery which has been hidden from ages and from generations but now has been revealed to His saints\ (Colossians 1:26)*

If we have the knowledge of God, we will be able to recognize the seasons as they unfold in the generations of our time until our Lord Jesus Christ appears and our hope for salvation through righteousness becomes real!

THE ELECT

These are the "set aside" ones (faithful to God) at the foundation of the earth (first world or earth age—Satan's revolt called katabole), which was when they stood with God against Satan, who caused the creation of the second earth age, or the flesh age.

There will be tribulation. Satan and the deceivers, who are the false teachers, will increase and lawlessness will abound. Love for one another will grow cold. The elects (sealed) will be hated for *"My Name's"* sake. The gospel of the kingdom will be preached. Pray to endure to the end, and you will be saved from the effects of Satan's tribulation.

Do not be deceived by Satan, who is coming at the sixth seal, sixth trump, and sixth vial (666). Wait for our Lord Jesus Christ at the last trump (777) when all will be turned into spirits. The seal of God in your mind (the knowledge of truth) will protect and guide you to stand firm on the Rock (Jesus Christ).

Those who are not deceived will continue to do God's work and will wait for the true Jesus Christ, who will be called "Our Husband" at the end of the millennium. We all who are sealed on earth as "overcomers" will assume our gender as female to become Jesus' "bride," after the great throne judgment. The wedding that is mentioned in the book of Revelation is Christ's marriage with His saints or the elect (Revelation 21:2).

It indicates that the elect or the chosen ones since the foundation had a destiny to serve Him.

> *Then I saw the Holy City, the new Jerusalem, coming down out of heaven from God, prepared as a bride adorned for her husband (Jesus). We, God's saints (in female gender), are the Lamb's wife, at the new heaven age, which is the eternity in the Holy city of Jerusalem. (Revelation 21:2,9)*

TEACHINGS ABOUT HEALTH LAWS

Foods allowed by God (clean animals)

Meat from animals that: "chews cud and has parted hoof and cloven footed"

1. Cow—Chews cud, parted hoof, and cloven footed.

2. Lamb—Chews cud, parted hoof, and cloven footed.

3. Deer— Chews cud, parted hoof, and cloven footed.

4. Turkey

5. Chicken

6. Fish that has scales—The scales protect the flesh of the fish that we eat from harmful substances.

Un-allowed foods (unclean):

1. Pig or swine – does not chew cud. (Lev. 11:7) The lowest type of animal that was absolutely meant to work as a "vacuum. cleaner" on earth, and therefore are unclean and unhealthy for human consumption.

2. Vulture and its kind (eagle, falcon, ostrich, hawk, kite, raven, owl, stork).

3. Hare

4. Mouse/rats/bats

5. Sea animals that have no scales.

6. Whatever crawls on its belly and animals that crawl on all fours (Leviticus 11:3)

LOVE

Love is a precious gift from God. Love is favored and approved by God. There is no violation of any law, and you do not commit sin when you walk with the fruits of the Holy Spirit, such as peace, hope, faith, joy, kindness, and other positive forces, nor be judged unrighteous with such.

It takes love and hope to believe God. To believe Him is faith. God is not pleased with us if we have no faith. All blessings flow from the LORD. He gives life, protection and guidance to do His will. He chose and directed prophets to teach us His truth.

> *"For God so loved the world, that He gave His only begotten Son that whoever believes in Him shall not perish but have everlasting life"* (*John 3:16*).

Love without hypocrisy in serving the Lord brings blessing. This is preached by the gospel.

"Honor all people, love the brotherhood" (1 Peter 2:17).

With sincere love (obeying the truth through the spirit) love one another with a pure heart.

"All of you be of one mind having compassion for one another. Love as brothers, be tender hearted, be courteous, not returning evil for evil or reviling for reviling, but blessing". (1 Peter 3:8-9)

Love will cover a multitude of sins. (1 Peter 4:8)

The spirit of love does not harm. Love is the fulfillment of the law, because with love for God we are blessed. There is no law governing, nor sin for judgment. With love, we get blessings.

PASSOVER

Passover is the feast of the unleavened bread. This is being celebrated to remind us that God saved the Israelites through Moses when he freed them from the slavery of the Egyptians. Jesus symbolizes the sacrificial lamb that was killed to redeem the people from their sins (Exodus 12:11). Jesus was with His twelve disciples before He died on the cross at the Last Supper to celebrate the Passover. Jesus took bread, blessed and broke it, and gave it to His disciples, and said:

"Take, eat: this is My body, broken for you. Do this in remembrance of Me". (Luke 22:19)

Then He took the cup and gave thanks and gave it to them. "Drink from it, all of you, for this is MY Blood of the new covenant which is shed for many for the remission of sins" (Matthew 26:28).

We usually celebrate Passover three times a year: beginning of Spring Equinox, typically falling on May 21, the Feast of Tabernacles, and the week of Jesus Christ's birthday, which is September 29, and at the Feast of Ingathering, which is at end of the year. However, there is no limit in time to celebrate Passover; we just have to avoid its becoming a "ritual practice."

SIN

All unrighteousness is sin. There is a sin that is not leading to death. Christ said, "Behold, all sins will be forgiven, the sons of man, and whatever blasphemies they may utter, but he who blasphemes against the Holy Spirit never has forgiven, but is subject to eternal condemnation" (Mark 3:28-29).

<u>The Unpardonable Sin</u> – When Satan and the anti-Christ will deliver you up to testify against them at the end times, do not premeditate what to say, but speak that whatever is given at that hour, for it is not you who speaks, but the Holy Spirit. Do not refuse the Holy Spirit because it is blasphemy and it is unpardonable.

Sin is defined as violation or transgression of God's law. Sin is the act of doing wrong. When you sin, you become unrighteous. God is unhappy when you commit sin. When you recognize you have sinned, you must repent with all sincerity. It follows, then, that you will have a new heart and therefore try not to sin again. Free yourself in your conscience of any guilt. As a person, the flesh is weak and tends to commit sin easily with so many temptations around us. Pray to God that if it becomes a habit it will eventually be stopped. If you have already asked for forgiveness upon repentance, do not bring it up again to God. He will be displeased because you appear to be making God a "liar" to forgive. Repent sincerely and try hard not to repeat the violating sin.

God is a "Cardio Knower." He will always forgive you if He can see in your heart that you are sincere. Be confident after repentance and move on to have a "fresh conscience."

Peter asked Jesus, "Lord, how often shall my brother sin against me, and I forgive him? Up to seven times?" (Matthew 18:21)

Jesus said to him, "I do not say to you, up to seven times, but up to seven times seventy (490 times)". That is a lot and more than enough!

My only two granddaughters, ages nine and five, are trained to apologize to anyone they have done wrong, and I am happy to say they know how to repent at an early age as they are growing up. Repentance is needed to be reconciled to God.

"As many as I love, I rebuke and chasten. Therefore be zealous and repent." (Revelation 3:19).

For Godly sorrow produces repentance to salvation, not to be regretted but the sorrow of the world produces death (2 Corinthians 7:10).

REPENTANCE AND FORGIVENESS

Forgiveness is a beautiful gift of God!

> *To the Lord, our God, belongs mercy and forgiveness though we have rebelled against Him. (Daniel 9:9)*

> *"And by Him (Jesus Christ) everyone who believes is justified from all things from which you could not be justified by the law of Moses (Acts 13:39)*

> *"But there is forgiveness with You. That you may be feared". (Psalm 130:4)*

I would fear Him for committing sin, but I will always remember to revere Him in my heart, because we have redemption through His blood, the forgiveness of sins according to the riches of His grace (Ephesians 1:7). With unrepentance, there is no forgiveness. According to God, if you forgive men of their trespasses, our heavenly Father will also forgive you. But if you do not forgive men their trespasses, neither will your Father forgive your trespasses (Matthew 6:14-15).

> *"The Lord is not slack [negligent] concerning His promise, as some counts slackness [slow or loose] but is long suffering [patient] toward us, not willing that anyone should perish but that all should come to repentance". (2 Peter 3:9)*

The Lord is very patient with all His children. He is very loving and merciful, and calls us to come to Him to repent of our sins and to be forgiven.

SEQUENCES OF EVENTS TO HAPPEN AT THE END OF THE AGES

(Signs of Jesus's coming—Matthew 24)

1. Jesus Christ warns us to beware of false apostles or prophets appearing in growing numbers using Christ's name. They are teaching traditions of man. Their words are full of lies and have no basis of truth.

2. Deceptions from false teachings that are misleading to people. This is our enemy at the end times.

3. Reports of news about wars and rumors of war and nation shall rise against nation, and kingdom against kingdom. Controversial issues and disagreements will cause problems that will lead to trouble among nations.

4. Occurrences of earthquakes, famines, and pestilences in many places of the world. Those disasters will surely bring sorrows. The gospel must be preached to warn us and be able to prepare ourselves mentally and spiritually, so we are not deceived.

5. Fearful sights in heaven are observed. There will be darkening of the earth due to diminishing lights coming from the sun, moon, and stars. Satan is about to come. People will be troubled and will panic. They are at a loss and get confused, especially those who have no knowledge, are, ignorant, or did not care to learn about God's truth. It is very important to know and understand God's message. He wrote to us by means of the Bible to prepare us for guidance and protection. The plagues and hard calamities are going to happen as warnings from God to call our attention! That is the reason why the gospel of God must be preached for teaching.

> *"Then they will deliver you up to tribulation and kill you and you will be hated by all nations for My Name's sake" (Matthew 24:9).*

6.   Satan and his fallen angels appear on earth because they were cast out of heaven by the archangel Michael when the armies of heaven defeated them in war. Satan was furious because he knows he has only a short time of five months. He goes after the children of God who are believers and sealed with God's knowledge. He will sit at the temple of God at Jerusalem and will claim himself to be God. He will come peacefully and prosperously. He will ensnare anyone with his weapon of lies and try very hard to deceive by smooth talking: to convince and tempt people with wondrous miracles, like snapping his fingers and will make fire or lightning appear from heaven. Many will be deceived. Jesus said, *"Watch for yourself. You will be arrested and delivered up as a testimony against them (the enemy)."* The Holy Spirit will help. *"Do not worry or premeditate what to speak, but what is given you in that hour, speak that: for it is not you who speak, but the Holy Spirit" (Mark 13:11).*

All people of any foreign language, or dialects of which you were born with, will come to understand. Satan will come peacefully and prosperously! He will offer some favors that would require free payments of house rentals, paying debts, availability of good food on the table for the family, secret deals, buying of votes, making contracts behind closed doors, making empty promises, just so he will be worshipped. All those are examples of his devious methods to make him accepted and worshipped. Many will be misled. The elect of God will not find him tempting, but an abomination to our Lord. Family members mwho are deceived will deliver their family members or friends to him thinking that he is the "true" Jesus or the "savior." Be careful to not be misguided! The elect of God were warned to be wise and let the seal of God (truth) in their minds be intact and to hold on to their faith with all diligence. They are always protected if they stand firm on the "Rock" (Jesus), they will not fear, and nothing will harm them.

> *Jesus said, "I gave you the authority to trample on serpents and scorpions and over all the power of the enemy and nothing shall by any means hurt you" (Luke10:19).*

> *The heavens and the earth will shake, but the Lord will be a shelter for His people and the strength of the children of Israel. (Joel 3:6)*

This means women who were deceived and are impregnated with Satan's teachings are warned about falling away from God.

Plagues and great disasters are coming as events of the difficult seasons ahead that will cause trouble in the whole world. The times of sufferings or hardships in life will come due to the tribulations caused by Satan.

Thank God! Those hard times are shortened for the elect's sake. Instead of seven years, it is shortened to five months by Jesus, lest no flesh will be able to survive. Just like in the days of Noah, before the flood, people were eating, drinking, marrying. and giving in marriage until the day that Noah entered the ark, and people did not know until the flood came and took them all away (Matthew 24:38-39).

Likewise, the fallen angels will come again at the end times to seduce women of their choice to become their wives.

> *Also, for this cause, ought the women to have a symbol of authority on her head [Jesus] because of the coming back of the fallen angels. (1 Corinthian 11:10)*

The power on the head as a covering (veil) symbolizes Jesus Christ, which means the knowledge that is sealed in her mind, spiritually speaking, should not be deceived, for it will be the same as it were in the beginning during Noah's time when the fallen angels came to deceive the earthly women to become their wives to produce giants as their offspring.

*7. At the last trumpet, Jesus will appear. Every knee shall bow to Him. This is the day of the Lord—the millennium—and at the end of the thousand years of His rule will be the judgment at the great white throne by our Almighty Father!

Author's Notes:

All is changed into spirit at the last trumpet. Jesus and His elect will teach for a thousand years, while Satan will be locked up in the abyss and will be released after that time. Those who were taught with God's truth will be tested and judged at the white throne judgment. Those who overcame will experience the second resurrection and be rewarded, while those who failed, because they will not accept the truth, will go into the lake of fire. The second resurrection indicates a good chance of hope for those who missed the first resurrection.

AION AGES
(The Heaven and World Ages)

It is believed by some religious leaders that this topic was not taught by churches because it is perceived as a controversial issue that would make worshippers doubt and draw them away from worshipping.

Know that there are three aion ages. This is the foundation of heaven and earth:

1. **The Spiritual Age** (foundation world)—The time when we were all with God in Spirit. It is the time when Satan revolted against God. One of God's most beautiful and wise sons, Lucifer (Satan's other name), revolted against God. He wanted to be like God. He pulled one-third of God's children to his side and caused them to follow him. God became very hurt and angry, so he destroyed that first earth age, and the earth became dark because our Father caused it to end (2 Peter 3:5-6).

    You who laid the foundation of the earth, so that it should not be moved forever, you covered it up as a garment. (Isaiah 51:13; 40:21)

2. **The Flesh Age** (this age)—The age we are living in now (the earth). God loves His children very much, so instead of killing the rest of his children, He allowed them to be born innocent through the womb of a woman in the second world age (Flesh Age). It is this earth where we now live, with a choice to love God or follow Satan. Satan has many different roles. He is tricky and very good to deceive people. God's Word in the Bible will teach us and warns us how not to be deceived and taken by him to perish at the end times in hell.

3. **The Eternal World Age** (is the new heaven)—This is the Eternity or Eternal World with God. Chapter 22 will give you more exciting information.

When we die, our spirits will return to the One who created us, our God. Our flesh is done with it. We are judged by our works according to what is written in the book of life.

When the flesh body dies, the dust will return to the earth as it was, and the spirit will return to God who gave it. (Genesis 3:19; Ecclesiastes 12:7)

"By the word of God, the heavens were of old, and the earth standing out of water, and in the water, by which the world that then existed perished, being flooded with water. But the heavens and the earth which now exist are kept in store by the same word, (God's words) reserved for fire until the judgement and perdition of ungodly men" (2 Peter 3:5).

In some museums and libraries there is information and printed pictures and artifacts, skeletal remains of dinosaurs, and other ancient mammals on display as evidenced by the many million years that happened before the flesh age.

For more information about the eternal world, read chapters 21 and 22 of the book of Revelation in this writing.

FALLEN ANGELS

The first world age was in heaven when Satan revolted against God. Satan pulled one-third of God's angels on his side to follow him. This event caused the destruction of that age, as God was grieved. Our Father destroyed everything except the angels who stood with Him while Satan's angels refused to leave their habitation but chose to come down to earth to seduce women of their choice and became their wives. They were called the fallen angels. God used all-natural methods to destroy that world by means of earthquakes, volcanoes, meteorites, and floods of waters that resulted in darkness.

The mixture of flesh bodies and angelic bodies resulted in the production of giant offspring. In Hebrew, it is called "Gibbor." Such mixture of offspring caused some human deformities, such as having six fingers on each hand, and six toes on each foot (Genesis 6:4).

Yet again there was battle in Gath, where there was a man of great stature, who had six fingers on each hand, and six toes on each foot, twenty-four in number; and he also was born to the giant (2 Samuel 21:20).

God allowed His remaining children to be born of a woman's womb, with a bag of water, and having no memory of the past that would give them a choice to follow Satan or love God. He would not allow His children to be destroyed because He loved them.

During the end times the coming of the fallen angels will alert women of earth again to remember that the veil on their head that is mentioned in the Bible is the power of Christ in their minds. They are not to be deceived.

> *"For this cause ought the women to have power on her head because of the angels". (1 Corinthians 11:10)*

The fallen angels are the ones mentioned here.

Maybe by that end time the seduction will not be physical seduction, but by a complete mental seduction of believing that Satan is the true Christ.

ADAM AND EVE

After God created everything for six days, He rested on the seventh day, and on the eighth day, He created the man, which in Hebrew is "Etha Adham," meaning "ruddy complexion liable to blush red in the face."

And the Lord had formed man of the dust of the ground and breathed into his nostrils the breath of life and he became a living soul. Adam was created (Genesis 2:1).

God took Adam to dress God's garden (Eden) and to take care of all that was is in the garden. Adam was not happy. He felt he needed help, but there was nothing he could find to make things better for him. He needed a companion, so God put him into a deep sleep and took the whitest tissue at the curved end of one of his ribs and made the woman, whose name was Eve. They became husband and wife, but they were both innocent. They were naked and unashamed (Genesis 3:20).

In these modern times, the white tissue that was taken from one end that is curved in Adam's rib is believed to be the helix curve that indicates the DNA today that is used in identifying a person in forensics.

And the Lord God instructed Adam, saying, "Of every tree of the garden, you may freely eat but the tree of the knowledge of good and evil, you shall not eat of it: for in the day that you do, you shall die" (Genesis 2:15-17).

Satan (the serpent mentioned in the Bible) lured Eve with cunning words of lies. Eve, who was innocent, was tempted and eventually was convinced, then finally denied God's instruction and followed Satan.

She was seduced by Satan and mated with him, then gave the forbidden fruit also to her husband. Finally, Eve was deceived together with her husband.

They became aware of their nakedness and felt ashamed with guilt in themselves. So, they sewed aprons out of the fig leaves to cover their private parts.

Never in the Bible was mentioned the fruit "apple" that is traditionally taught by man.

When God found out that Adam and Eve had disobeyed His instruction about eating from the tree of the knowledge of good and evil, He said to Satan, "I will put enmity between thee and the woman, and between thy seed and her seed, it shall bruise His heel, and unto the woman, He said I will greatly multiply thy sorrow, thou shalt bring forth children; and thy desire shall be to thy husband and he shall rule over thee" (Genesis 3:14-16).

To the serpent, or Satan, he said: "Because thou have done this, thou art cursed above all cattle, and above every beast of the field: upon thy belly shall thou go, and dust shall thou eat all the days of thy life."

To Adam, God said, "Because you have heeded the voice of your wife and had eaten from the tree of which I commanded you saying, you shall not eat of it, nor shall you touch it, lest you die. Cursed is the ground for your sake; in toil you shall eat of it all the days of your life. Both thorns and thistles it shall bring forth for you, and you shall eat the herbs of the field. In the sweat of your face, you shall eat bread until you shall return to the ground."

Men die in the flesh because of disobedience to God's Word as revealed in the Bible.

EVE'S CONCEPTION

All along, Satan knew that it was through Eve's bloodline that Christ would come. So, Satan took advantage of Eve's innocence to destroy God's plan and went ahead to plant "his seed" into the womb of Eve.

Seed means "posterity, or the successive generation of a person not yet born." This is Satan's method of deception to take advantage of us if we don't understand God's plan. We must be wiser than him.

So, Eve got pregnant and conceived with twins: Cain and Abel were fraternal twins, which means the seed of Satan produced Cain, and the seed of Adam produced Abel.

There are two kinds of twins. Twins are born of the same day:

1. Identical twins—conception takes place with fertilization and subsequent splitting of an egg or a single ovum and share the same bag of water throughout the pregnancy, and the babies look exactly alike. (God puts different souls in each fetus.)

2. Fraternal twins—come from two separate eggs, or ova, from the womb and are fertilized anywhere from two to six weeks of pregnancy, then will have their own bag of waters, and can have two fathers, just like Cain and

Abel. The babies can look different and can have the same or opposite sex (medical explanation for this is needed to be proven).

In the process of time, when the twins grew up, Cain became a tiller of the ground, and Abel a keeper of sheep. When they were of age to make an offering to God for their blessing, Cain brought fruit of the ground, and Abel brought the best of his firstlings of his flocks and of the fat thereof. And the Lord had respect unto Abel and his offering, but Cain and unto his offering, He had not respect. And Cain was very wrought, and his countenance fell (Genesis 4:3-5).

God told Cain if he would have been honest and given God his best, He would have accepted Cain's offering. So out of his rage, Cain murdered Abel.

God drove Cain away to be a fugitive and a vagabond on the earth. Cain foresaw and complained that whoever would find him would slay him. But God said that whoever will kill Cain would be avenged seven -fold. And so, the Lord set a mark on Cain lest anyone who found him would kill him.

Cain went to the land of Nod and married a woman created by God on the sixth day of creation. Now Cain and his descendants (the Kenites) would carry out the negative part of God's plan. The "mark" the Lord placed on Cain would be the beginning of the mark of the beast in the book of Revelation. It begins with the seed line with Cain as the first murderer.

And Adam knew his wife again, and she bore a son and called his name Seth. Seth was born as a substitute to Abel. For God the word "Seth" means substitution. This bloodline that began in Seth would continue all the way through history until Christ would finally come (Genesis 4:25).

BODIES

We have two bodies. Your soul is yourself. And your spirit is the intellect of your soul. "And do not fear those who kill the body but cannot kill the soul. But rather fear Him who is able to destroy both soul and body in hell." (Matthew 10:28)

"We are confident, yes, well pleased rather to be absent from the body and to be present with the Lord." (2 Corinthians 5:8)

1. Physical body—that which is your flesh or natural body. It is made of flesh, muscles, bones, blood, etc., which can be seen: this flesh body dies, and it is corruptible. It gets sick, old, and wrinkled. Eventually, it will die.

2. Spiritual body—upon death of the flesh body, the soul and spirit are inside our flesh body and cannot be seen. It goes back to the Father, our God who gave it. It is a better body because it does not grow old and sick, or experience any pain or sufferings. This spiritual body can be incorruptible or immortal (deathlessness), or mortal (liable to die) both. All souls will be facing God at judgement time.

The physical body or the natural body was originally made out of clay. When it dies, it is compared to a seed. It is sown to the ground and will germinate and becomes an alive plant. The flesh body when it dies, goes to the ground and becomes dust unless God will accept it as a spirit because flesh and blood which is a corrupt body cannot enter in heaven unless it is raised to incorruption (deathlessness).

At the last trumpet we shall all be changed to spirit. The dead will change from corruptible and be raised to incorruption, and the mortal body must put on immortality (deathlessness). And so "death is swallowed up in victory" (1 Corinthians 15:44).

The victory is accounted for our Lord, Jesus Christ. Through His death on the cross, He was able to defeat death, who is Satan (Hebrews 2:14).

Satan

Satan is the wicked one. He was an angel of God (cherub) that at the foundation of the world was created with a seal of perfection, full of wisdom and perfect beauty. He was overwhelmingly spoiled by God. However, he held a super ego and became arrogant and prideful. He became a very wicked angel and revolted against God.

"You corrupted your wisdom with your prideful and wicked training, and I turned you into ashes upon the earth. You became a horror and shall be no more forever" (Ezekiel 28:12).

He is the only one who has already been judged to die and will surely be sent to the lake of fire.

"How you are fallen from heaven Lucifer, son of the morning, how you were cut down to the ground. You, who weakened the nations! You have said in your heart: 'I will ascend into heaven, I will exalt my throne above the stars of God; I will also sit on the mount of the congregation on the farthest sides of the North; I will ascend above the heights of the clouds, I will be like the Most High, yet you shall be brought down to Sheol, to the lowest depths of the pit" (Isaiah 14:12-13).

Satan is the only soul that has already been judged to die.

SATAN'S VARIOUS NAMES

1. The Serpent—Revelation 12:9: "So the great dragon was cast out that serpent of old called the devil and Satan, who deceives the whole world; he was cast to the earth, and his angels were cast out with him."

2. Dragon—Referred to as the "great dragon".

3. Devil—Satan is also the devil.

4. Lucifer—"How you are fallen from heaven Lucifer, son of the morning." (Isaiah 14:12-13)

5. Son of Perdition—"Let no one deceive you, by any means; for that Day will not come unless the falling away comes first, and the man of sin is revealed, the son of perdition who opposes and exalt himself above all that is called God or that is worshipped so that he sits as God in the temple of God, showing himself that he is God." (2 Thessalonians 2:3)

6. Evil Spirit—And Saul's servants said to him, "Surely, a distressing spirit from God is troubling you." (1 Samuel 16:15)

7. Power of darkness (Satan has always been identified with darkness)—" Those who sat in darkness and in the shadow of death, bound in affliction and irons—because they rebelled against the words of God, and despised the counsel of the Most High," (Psalms 107:10)

8. Abaddon (In Hebrew)—And they had as king over them the angel of the bottomless pit, whose name in Hebrew is Abaddon. But in Greek, he has the name Apollyon. (Revelation 9:11)

9. Apollyon – Satan's name in Greek.

10. Death—"Knowing that Christ, having been raised from the dead, dies no more. Death no longer has dominion over Him." (Romans 6:9). Jesus was crucified to defeat death (Hebrew 2:14).

11. Beast—"The beast that you saw was, and is not, and will ascend out of the bottomless pit and go to perdition. And those who dwell on the earth will marvel, whose names are not written in the Book of Life from the foundation of the world, when they see the beast that was, and is not, and yet is." (Revelation 17:8)

12. Anti-Christ—(Instead of Christ). "Little children, it is the last hour; and as you have heard the Antichrist is coming, even now, many antichrists have come, by which we know that it is the last hour." (1 John 2:18)

13. Accuser—Then I heard a voice saying in heaven, "now salvation, and strength, and the kingdom or our God and the power of His Christ have come for the Accuser of our brethren, who accused them before our God day and night, has been cast down. (Revelation 12:10)

14. Destroyer—"The lion has come up from his thicket, and the Destroyer of nations is on his way. He has gone forth from his place to make your land desolate. Your cities will be laid waste, without inhabitant." (Jeremiah 4:7)

15. Prince of Tyre/King of Tyre—(Behold you are wiser than Daniel): "There is no secret that can be hidden from you. With your wisdom and understanding, you have gained riches for yourself, and gathered gold and silver into your treasuries; by your great wisdom in trade, you have

increased your riches, and your heart is lifted up because of your riches" (Ezekiel 28:2-19).

During the ancient times, the seat of commerce of all cities was in a certain island in Philistia called Tyre. They made trades of commerce in many costal lands with all precious things in that place. Great trade and commerce are mentioned and assumed by the prince and king of Tyre.

SATAN AS DESCRIBED BY GOD

"Son of man, take up a lamentation for the king of Tyre, and say to him, 'Thus says the Lord God:

"You were the seal of perfection, Full of wisdom and perfect in beauty. You were in Eden, the garden of God; Every precious stone was your covering: The sardius, topaz, and diamond, Beryl, onyx, and jasper, sapphire, turquoise, and emerald with gold. The workmanship of your timbrels and pipes was prepared for you on the day you were created. "You *were* the anointed cherub who covers; I established you;

You were on the holy mountain of God; You walked back and forth in the midst of fiery stones (precious stones).

You *were* perfect in your ways from the day you were created, Till iniquity was found in you. "By the abundance of your trading You became filled with violence within, And you sinned; Therefore I cast you as a profane thing out of the mountain of God; And I destroyed you, O covering cherub, From the midst of the fiery stones. "Your heart was lifted up because of your beauty; You corrupted your wisdom forthe sake of your splendor; I cast you to the ground, I laid you before kings, That they might gaze at you.

""You defiled your sanctuaries by the multitude of your iniquities, by the iniquity of your trading;

Therefore I brought fire from your midst; It devoured you, And I turned you to ashes upon the earth

In the sight of all who saw you. All who knew you among the peoples are astonished at you; You have become a horror, And shall be no more forever.""" (Ezekiel 28:12-19)

NOAH'S FLOOD

It is stated that: The rebellion of Satan caused the destruction of the first world age. God was very hurt and angry. Instead of killing His children, whom He loved, He allowed His children to be born of a woman in the womb with a bag of waters and to be born innocent (no memory of the past), and later given a choice whether to follow Satan or love God. The one-third of angels on Satan's side were called the fallen angels. They could not wait for God to make them born of a woman, so they instead refused to leave their habitation and went down to earth and seduced women, took them as wives, and then conceived and bore giants. During those times the world became polluted and perversion prevailed. So, God looked at Noah and considered him just and perfect in that generation. He instructed Noah to build an ark with measurements for the windows and doors, and to make three decks (Genesis 6:17, Genesis 9:15).

God said, "I am bringing the flood of waters to the earth to destroy from under heaven. All flesh and everything will die. But I will establish my covenant with you and you shall go into the ark. You, your wife, and your sons, and your son's wives and of every living thing of all flesh, you shall bring two of every sort into the ark, and to keep them alive, they shall be made male and female, of the birds after their kind and animals after their kind, and of every creeping thing of the earth after each kind, two of every kind will come to you and to keep them alive."

> *"You shall take with you seven each of every clean animal, with a male and his female, two each of animals that are unclean, a male and female. Also, seven each of birds of the air, male and female, to keep this species alive in the face of all the earth. For after seven days I will cause it to rain on the earth. Forty days and forty nights, I will destroy from the face of the earth all living things that I have made." (Genesis 7:2-24)*

Noah did according to all that the Lord commanded him. And after seven days, there came the flood on earth, and the heavy rain was on the earth forty days and forty nights.

The waters increased and lifted the ark, and it rose high above the earth. And the mountains were covered, and all flesh died. Only Noah and those who were with him in the ark remained alive. The waters prevailed on the earth one hundred fifty days. The waters were finally restrained. On the seventh month and seventeenth day of the month, the ark rested on the mountains of Ararat. Slowly, the waters abated from the earth and the waters dried up. God said to Noah and all with him in the ark: "Bring out with you and your wife and your sons and your son's wives, also bring out with you every living thing of all flesh, birds, and cattle and every creeping thing that creeps on the earth, so that they may abound on the earth." So, Noah and all went out of the ark. He built an altar to the Lord and took of every clean bird and offered burnt offerings on the altar. And the Lord smelled a soothing aroma, then the Lord said in His heart, "I will never again curse theground for man's sake. Although the imagination of man's heart is evil from his youth, nor will I again destroy every living thing as I have done. I set my rainbow in the cloud, and it shall be for the sign of the covenant between Me and the earth."

So, God blessed Noah and his sons and said to them, "Be fruitful and multiply, fill the earth."

After all these things happened, thus all races were created by God.

MOSES AND LAWS

He was a great prophet of God who led the Hebrews out of bondage from the cruelty of the Egyptians. Also, through him, the Ten Commandments of God were given to the people to be spread to the whole world. He was a great leader teaching the Word of God. The Ten Commandments of God are laws that people now believe that our Constitution was patterned after. Then, there are various important laws that were formed from the time of Moses written in the books of Deuteronomy and Leviticus that are approved by God, which are important in our lives these days to follow like the health laws and moral laws. If we break any of the laws in the Bible, surely there are consequences that are troubles for us. Passover was introduced during the time of Moses.

During his time, many plagues were laid out by God with Moses warning Pharaoh and the Egyptians about it. But each time a plague happened, the Egyptians were indignant to follow Moses' warnings, each time a plague comes, the Pharaoh summons Moses and Aaron for help to restore the Egyptians' lives to normal with promise to obey. They ignored the warnings until finally it piled up, and in the end, they could hardly tolerate it any longer. Pharaoh eventually agreed to let them go free after the last plaque, which killed all the firstborn. Meanwhile, Passover was instituted led by Moses. They celebrated the feast of the unleavened bread with instructions. The Passover became a feast to be celebrated by eating unleavened bread. God commanded Moses to kill an unblemished lamb to be roasted in the evening to eat. The blood of the killed lamb must be put (as a stain) on the doorposts and lintels of the houses as they eat so that the death angel will see and pass over the houses of the families, and their firstborn would be safe from the death plague that God had laid on the Egyptians.

In the meantime, the Hebrews were preparing in haste to leave Egypt as commanded by God. So, they did not have time to make their dough to rise. They packed up their things and their unleavened dough. In the present, it is significant that the slain lamb was symbolic of Jesus Christ, who became our Passover to save us from our sins (1 Corinthian 5:7).

The Red Sea was parted miraculously by God to let the Hebrews cross over as if they were walking on dry land. And when the Egyptian army tried to pursue them with their chariots, all of them drowned.

The Ten Commandments of God were given to Moses to teach to the people until the time of Jesus Christ's ministry, in which we were given a gift of love that through His grace, repentance and forgiveness were preached, which is necessary for our salvation.

A Brief Story About
King David
1 Samuel 16:12-13 (up to the book of Kings)

King David was a great hero and character as told about in the Bible. He was a man who was loved and blessed by the Lord. He became a great king from being a shepherd. He was always faithful with God. All his life as king, he was engaged in battlefields and wars that exalted his kingdom in Israel for God's people. He must have killed thousands and thousands of enemies.

When he was just a boy of twelve years, he was a shepherd of his father's flocks of sheep. He trained himself to be a strong fighter of lions and bears that would take a sheep. He was the youngest son among eight siblings of his father, Jesse. He became famous as the hero who fought and killed the champion and leader Goliath, the giant of the Philistines. He was described as a young man of valor, a man of war with prudent speech, very handsome with a ruddy face, bright eyes, and a very good-looking person.

The king at that time was King Saul, who promised that whoever could kill the Philistine leader would receive the prize of honor and riches and be given the privilege of marrying King Saul's daughter. And so, he became a great king after killing Goliath. The people rejoiced and loved David.

Being faithful to the Lord, David was always guided and blessed by God. He was just a youth when he could not bear hearing the mocking, abuses, and maltreatment of the Philistines. He accepted the challenge of Goliath, who disdained him terribly, saying that whoever among the Israelites could defeat him, they would all become their servants.

All through his life, David did not allow himself to be influenced by any religious beliefs or worshiping false gods or following false teachings.

He also made some mistakes in his life that made God feel displeased in His eyes. And he had to accept and suffer some punishment from God.

One of his sons, Nathan, brought the generational seed line to Jesus Christ (Jesus was the root and offspring of David (Revelation 5:5). Also, the great King Solomon was one of his sons who succeeded him, and was very famous for his great wisdom.

King David was king of Hebron for seven and a half years and reigned King in Jerusalem for thirty-three years. He had a total of nineteen sons from different wives and one daughter; besides, he had many concubines.

KING SOLOMON'S BOOK OF
ECCLESIASTES

The book of Ecclesiastes is written by King Solomon, one of King David's son who was blessed by God with wealth, great knowledge, and wisdom. With his wonderful experience, he shares in this book as a preacher. He tells how to live happily and healthy on this earth. God allows us to live actively to experience and work for a living, how to have knowledge, to develop skills, and how to acquire wisdom to be successful. But from all these advantages, we must not forget our responsibility to acknowledge God's love for us as His children. Keep God's commandments for there will always be a time for judgement.

God must not be feared but revered (loved). We must rejoice in our good works because it is our heritage from God. However, King Solomon says death comes to all! Everything is vanity (empty) because the true value and meaning of life are only found in God. We are blessed if we do things right. God will judge the righteous as well as the wicked. We shall all die to face Him on judgment day. We are judged according to our works (Revelation 19:8).

Some examples of righteous works are: love God by doing good deeds: taking care of family, or respecting the rights of any person. The elect's main mission is not to premeditate what to say when they are delivered up to testify against the enemy, but to speak that what is given to them at the hour of temptation to allow the Holy Spirit to speak through them so that all people will hear and understand the Message of God. This is the sign of the Holy Spirit speaking in cloven tongues in many different dialects and languages at one time and all nations will understand.

According to King Solomon, there is nothing to fear because God is merciful, and if we truly repent of our sins, the grace of forgiveness is granted through Jesus Christ, His Son, if you ask. Furthermore, he says there is nothing better for a man to do but eat, drink, and enjoy his labor. It is a gift of God (Ecclesiastes 3:13).

A Brief Story Of Job

Job was among the sons of God in the first world age. He was a good example of someone who was persecuted by Satan.

When he lived on earth (flesh), his faith with God was strong, and God's blessings were with Him. He was a pious and very rich man. However, he suffered many hardships to test his faith. He was persecuted by Satan, as challenged by God to Satan, or allowed by God to attack him (but not to kill him). He lost all his worldly goods and was afflicted by a terrible disease. Three among his friends came to sympathize with his sufferings. About thirty-eight long chapters discussed in the book of Job, they insisted that Job must have sinned greatly against God because of his misery (Read page 4).

Job was very indignant and sure that what they were accusing him of was not true. Even his wife was mad at him after losing all his valuable things in life that she even cursed him to die. With his misery, he eagerly wanted to see and talk to God. When God confronted him, he was made to admit that his wisdom was not good enough to dominate or override God's wisdom. Finally, he humbled himself with sincerity, and with his new behavior, he found stronger faith, regained his health, wealth, and peace. God restored all his wealth, even more than what he had (Job 38).

THE TRUTH ABOUT
THE "RAPTURE" OR "FLY
AWAY" THEORY

The word "rapture" is not even found in the bible. It is a false teaching that started in 1832 when an ill woman made up a false belief from her dream that we are going to fly away like birds toward our salvation to meet the Lord in the air. This is completely a false teaching that was witnessed by two ministers at her bedside and spread the false message. God is against this teaching.

> *"Behold, I am against your magic charms by which you hunt souls there like birds. I will tear them from your arms, and let the souls go, the souls you hunt like birds. I will also tear off your veils and deliver My people out of your hand, and they shall no longer be as prey in your hand. Then you shall know that I am the Lord". (Ezekiel 13:20-21)*

These two issues are beliefs that are mostly confusing to people who read the Bible in 1 Thessalonian 4:14-17. To better understand the chapters, you must begin and focus your reading from verse 13 first, and then follow it up in 1 Corinthian 15:51-53, which explains about "the day of the Lord." Now here, as described, it is self-explanatory.

"But I do not want you to be ignorant, brethren, concerning those who have <u>fallen asleep</u> [died] lest you sorrow as others who have no hope. For if we believe that Jesus died and rose again, even so, God will bring with Him those who sleep in Jesus [They have gone to heaven]. For this we say to you by the word of the Lord, that we who are alive and remain until the coming of the Lord will by no means precede those who are asleep [<u>died and are already in paradise, the waiting place in heaven</u>]. For the Lord Himself will descend from heaven with a shout, with the voice of an archangel, and with the last trumpet of God. All is changed into spirit. And the dead in Christ will rise first. Then we who are alive and remain shall be caught up together with them in the clouds [expression like clouds of birds] to meet the Lord in the air [breath of life]. And thus we shall always be with the Lord. (1 Thessalonian 4:13-17)

Those who have died in Jesus have already gone to paradise with Him. We who are alive will be caught up with them and will meet the Lord at the sound of the seventh trumpet in a new life when He appears.

AUTHOR'S NOTES:

After the last trumpet sounds, we shall all be changed to spirits: "Behold I tell you a mystery: we shall not all sleep, but we shall all be changed in a moment, in the twinkling of an eye, the last trumpet will sound. For the trumpet will sound, and the dead will be raised incorruptible, and we shall be changed. For this corruptible body [flesh body] must put on incorruption and this mortal body (liable to die) must put on immortality [deathlessness]." (1 Corinthians 15:51-53).

When Satan comes to earth to play the role of Jesus, he will say, "I come to fly you away to save your souls." This is a method of deceiving the people to worship him. It is only through Jesus Christ that we can be saved. Remember He died on the cross for our sake, for us to be saved. Don't be deceived with Satan's big lies, misleading words, and his display of wonder miracles, such as snapping his fingers and causing fire or lightning to fall from heaven. God's message is always to be strong with your faith, having the seal of the knowledge of God in your minds so you will not be misled.

Traditions Of Man

This denies the Word of God (Mark 7:13).

"for prophecy never came by the will of man, but holy men of God spoke as they were moved by the Holy Spirit" (2 Peter 1:21)

False prophets use destructive heresies that blaspheme, but they will be destroyed in the end.

For if God did not spare the angels who sinned, but cast *them* down to hell and delivered *them* into chains of darkness, to be reserved for judgment; (2 Peter 2:4)

God will judge those who live ungodly, and, just as the false prophets, they will be destroyed in the end.

For such are false apostles, deceitful workers transforming (disguised) themselves into apostles of Christ. And no wonder: For Satan himself will transform into an angel of light. (2 Corinthians 11:13)

This is truly called blasphemy, which is very repulsive, absolute contrary to the truth and therefore deserves to be included in God's wrath.

God loves His children, especially those who are strong in faith and are willing to serve Him.

God did not appoint us to wrath but to obtain salvation through our Lord Jesus Christ. (1 Thessalonians 5:9)

God's wrath will be brought upon the many hoaxes and manipulations to bring deceptions and lies by the anti-Christ and Satan's army.

Faithful and righteous people of God who have the seal of truth are protected and standing safely with the Rock, who is our Savior. Love the Lord and recognize those who teach the true words of God.

THE REVELATION OF
JESUS CHRIST

1 The Revelation of Jesus Christ, which God gave Him to show His servants—things which must shortly take place. And He sent and signified it by His angel to His servant John, ² who bore witness to the word of God, and to the testimony of Jesus Christ, to all things that he saw. ³ Blessed is he who reads and those who hear the words of this prophecy, and keep those things which are written in it; for the time is near.

<u>The Seven Churches</u>

⁴ John, to the seven churches which are in Asia:

Grace to you and peace from Him who is and who was and who is to come, and from the seven Spirits who are before His throne, ⁵ and from Jesus Christ, the faithful witness, the firstborn from the dead, and the ruler over the kings of the earth.

To Him who loved us and washed us from our sins in His own blood, ⁶ and has made us kings and priests to His God and Father, to Him be glory and dominion forever and ever. Amen.

⁷ Behold, He is coming with clouds, and every eye will see Him, even they who pierced Him. And all the tribes of the earth will mourn because of Him. Even so, Amen.

⁸ "I am the Alpha and the Omega, *the* Beginning and the End," says the Lord, "who is and who was and who is to come, the Almighty."

⁹ I, John, both your brother and companion in the tribulation and kingdom and patience of Jesus Christ, was on the island that is called Patmos for the word of God and for the testimony of Jesus Christ. ¹⁰ I was in the Spirit on the Lord's Day, and I heard behind me a loud voice, as of a trumpet, ¹¹ saying, "I am the Alpha and the Omega, the First and the Last," and,[f] "What you see, write in a book and send it to the seven churches which are in Asia:[g] to Ephesus, to Smyrna, to Pergamos, to Thyatira, to Sardis, to Philadelphia, and to Laodicea."

¹² Then I turned to see the voice that spoke with me. And having turned I saw seven golden lampstands, ¹³ and in the midst of the seven lampstands\ One like the Son of Man, clothed with a garment down to the feet and girded about the chest with a golden band. ¹⁴ His head and hair were white like wool, as white as snow, and His eyes like a flame of fire; ¹⁵ His feet were like fine brass, as if refined in a furnace, and His voice as the sound of many waters; ¹⁶ He had in His right hand seven stars, out of His mouth went a sharp two-edged sword, and His countenance was like the sun shining in its strength. ¹⁷ And when I saw Him, I fell at His feet as dead. But He laid His right hand on me, saying to me, "Do not be afraid; I am the First and the Last. ¹⁸ I am He who lives, and was dead, and behold, I am alive forevermore. Amen. And I have the keys of Hades and of Death. ¹⁹ Write the things which you have seen, and the things which are, and the things which will take place after this. ²⁰ The mystery of the seven stars which you saw in My right hand, and the seven golden lampstands: The seven stars are the angels of the seven churches, and the seven lampstands which you saw[j] are the seven churches.

2 "To the angel of the church of **Ephesus** write, 'These things says He who holds the seven stars in His right hand, who walks in the midst of the seven golden lampstands: ² "I know your works, your labor, your patience, and that you cannot bear those who are evil. And you have tested those who say they are apostles and are not and have found them liars; ³ and you have persevered and have patience and have labored for My name's sake and have not become weary. ⁴ Nevertheless I have this against you, that you have left your first love. ⁵ Remember therefore from where you have fallen; repent and do the first works, or else I will come to you quickly and remove your lampstand from its place—unless you repent. ⁶ But this you have, that you hate the deeds of the Nicolaitans, which I also hate.

⁷ "He who has an ear, let him hear what the Spirit says to the churches. To him who overcomes I will give to eat from the tree of life, which is in the midst of the Paradise of God.'"

⁸ "And to the angel of the church in **Smyrna** write, 'These things says the First and the Last, who was dead, and came to life: ⁹ "I know your works, tribulation, and poverty (but you are rich); and *I know* the blasphemy of those who say they are Jews and are not but are a synagogue of Satan. ¹⁰ Do not fear any of those things which you are about to suffer. Indeed, the devil is about to throw some of you into prison, that you may be

tested, and you will have tribulation ten days. Be faithful until death, and I will give you the crown of life.

[11] "He who has an ear, let him hear what the Spirit says to the churches. He who overcomes shall not be hurt by the second death.'"

[12] "And to the angel of the church in **Pergamos** write,
'These things says He who has the sharp two-edged sword: [13] "I know your works, and where you dwell, where Satan's throne is. And you hold fast to My name and did not deny My faith even in the days in which Antipas *was* My faithful martyr, who was killed among you, where Satan dwells. [14] But I have a few things against you, because you have there those who hold the doctrine of Balaam, who taught Balak to put a stumbling block before the children of Israel, to eat things sacrificed to idols, and to commit sexual immorality. [15] Thus you also have those who hold the doctrine of the Nicolaitans, which thing I hate. [16] Repent, or else I will come to you quickly and will fight against them with the sword of My mouth.

[17] "He who has an ear, let him hear what the Spirit says to the churches. To him who overcomes I will give some of the hidden manna to eat. And I will give him a white stone, and on the stone a new name written which no one knows except him who receives *it*.'"

[18] "And to the angel of the church in **Thyatira** write,
'These things says the Son of God, who has eyes like a flame of fire, and His feet like fine brass: [19] "I know your works, love, service, faith, and your patience; and as for your works, the last are more than the first. [20] Nevertheless I have a few things against you, because you allow that woman Jezebel, who calls herself a prophetess, to teach and seduce My servants to commit sexual immorality and eat things sacrificed to idols. [21] And I gave her time to repent of her sexual immorality, and she did not repent. [22] Indeed I will cast her into a sickbed, and those who commit adultery with her into great tribulation, unless they repent of their deeds. [23] I will kill her children with death, and all the churches shall know that I am He who searches the minds and hearts. And I will give to each one of you according to your works.

[24] "Now to you I say, and to the rest in Thyatira, as many as do not have this doctrine, who have not known the depths of Satan, as they say, I will put on you no other burden. [25] But hold fast what you have till I come. [26] And he who overcomes, and keeps My works until the end, to him I will give power over the nations— [27] 'He shall rule them with a rod of iron; They shall be dashed to pieces like the potter's vessels'— as I also have received from My Father; 28 and I will give him the morning star.

[29] "He who has an ear, let him hear what the Spirit says to the churches.'"

3 "And to the angel of the church in **Sardis** write, 'These things says He who has the seven Spirits of God and the seven stars: "I know your works, that you have a name that you are alive, but you are dead. 2 Be watchful, and strengthen the things which remain, that are ready to die, for I have not found your works perfect before God. 3 Remember therefore how you have received and heard; hold fast and repent. Therefore, if you will not watch, I will come upon you as a thief, and you will not know what hour I will come upon you. 4 You have a few names even in Sardis who have not defiled their garments; and they shall walk with Me in white, for they are worthy. 5 He who overcomes shall be clothed in white garments, and I will not blot out his name from the Book of Life; but I will confess his name before My Father and before His angels.

6 "He who has an ear, let him hear what the Spirit says to the churches.'"

7 "And to the angel of the church in **Philadelphia** write, 'These things says He who is holy, He who is true, "He who has the key of David, He who opens, and no one shuts, and shuts and no one opens": 8 "I know your works. See, I have set before you an open door, and no one can shut it; for you have a little strength, have kept My word, and have not denied My name. 9 Indeed I will make *those* of the synagogue of Satan, who say they are Jews and are not, but lie— indeed I will make them come and worship before your feet, and to know that I have loved you. 10 Because you have kept My command to persevere, I also will keep you from the hour of trial which shall come upon the whole world, to test those who dwell on the earth. 11 Behold, I am coming quickly! Hold fast what you have, that no one may take your crown.12 He who overcomes, I will make him a pillar in the temple of My God, and he shall go out no more. I will write on him the name of My God and the name of the city of My God, the New Jerusalem, which comes down out of heaven from My God. And *I will write on him* My new name.

13 "He who has an ear, let him hear what the Spirit says to the churches.'"

14 "And to the angel of the church of the Laodiceans write, 'These things says the Amen, the Faithful and True Witness, the Beginning of the creation of God: 15 "I know your works, that you are neither cold nor hot. I could wish you were cold or hot. 16 So then, because you are lukewarm, and neither cold nor hot, I will vomit you out of My mouth. 17 Because you say, 'I am rich, have become wealthy, and have need of nothing'—and do not know that you are wretched, miserable, poor, blind, and naked— 18 I counsel you to buy from Me gold refined in the fire, that you may be rich; and white garments, that you may be clothed, that the shame of your nakedness may not be revealed; and anoint your eyes with eye salve, that you may see. 19 As many as I love, I rebuke and chasten. Therefore, be zealous and repent. 20 Behold, I stand at the door and knock. If anyone hearsMy voice and opens the door, I will come in to him and dine with him, and he with Me. 21 To him who overcomes I will grant to sit with Me on My throne, as I also overcame and sat down with My Father on His throne.

22 "He who has an ear, let him hear what the Spirit says to the churches.'""

4 After this I looked, and there before me was a door standing open in heaven. And the voice I had first heard speaking to me like a trumpet said, "Come up here, and I will show you what must take place after this." [2] At once I was in the Spirit, and there before me was a throne in heaven with someone sitting on it. [3] And the one who sat there had the appearance of jasper and ruby. A rainbow that shone like an emerald encircled the throne. [4] Surrounding the throne were twenty-four other thrones and seated on them were twenty-four elders. They were dressed in white and had crowns of gold on their heads. [5] From the throne came flashes of lightning, rumblings and peals of thunder. In front of the throne, seven lamps were blazing. These are the seven spirits[a] of God. [6] Also in front of the throne there was what looked like a sea of glass, clear as crystal. In the center, around the throne, were four living creatures, and they were covered with eyes, in front and in back. [7] The first living creature was like a lion, the second was like an ox, the third had a face like a man, the fourth was like a flying eagle. [8] Each of the four living creatures had six wings and was covered with eyes all around, even under its wings. Day and night, they never stop saying:

"'Holy, holy, holy
is the Lord God Almighty,
who was, and is, and is to come."

[9] Whenever the living creatures give glory, honor and thanks to him who sits on the throne and who lives for ever and ever, [10] the twenty- four elders fall down before him who sits on the throne and worship him who lives for ever and ever. They lay their crowns before the throne and say:

[11] "You are worthy, our Lord and God, to receive glory and honor and power, for you created all things, and by your will they were created and have their being."

5 Then I saw in the right hand of him who sat on the throne a scroll with writing on both sides and sealed with seven seals. [2] And I saw a mighty angel proclaiming in a loud voice, "Who is worthy to break the seals and open the scroll?" [3] But no one in heaven or on earth or under the earth could open the scroll or even look inside it. [4] I wept and wept because no one was found who was worthy to open the scroll or look inside. [5] Then one of the elders said to me, "Do not weep! See, the Lion of the tribe of Judah, the Root of David, has triumphed. He is able to open the scroll and its seven seals."

[6] Then I saw a Lamb, looking as if it had been slain, standing at the center of the throne, encircled by the four living creatures and the elders. The Lamb had seven horns and seven eyes, which are the seven spirits of God sent out into all the earth. [7] He went and took the scroll from the right hand of him who sat on the throne. [8] And when he had taken it, the four living creatures and the twenty-four elders fell down before the Lamb. Each one had a harp and they were holding golden bowls full of incense, which are the prayers of God's people. [9] And they sang a new song, saying:

"You are worthy to take the scroll and to open its seals, because you were slain, and with your blood you purchased for God persons from every tribe and language and people and nation.

[10] You have made them to be a kingdom and priests to serve our God, and they will reign on the earth."

[11] Then I looked and heard the voice of many angels, numbering thousands upon thousands, and ten thousand times ten thousand. They encircled the throne and the living creatures and the elders. [12] In a loud voice they were saying:

"Worthy is the Lamb, who was slain, to receive power and wealth and wisdom and strength and honor and glory and praise!"

[13] Then I heard every creature in heaven and on earth and under the earth and on the sea, and all that is in them, saying: "To him who sits on the throne and to the Lamb be praise and honor and glory and power, for ever and ever!"

[14] The four living creatures said, "Amen," and the elders fell down and worshiped.

AUTHOR'S NOTES:

THE REVELATION OF JESUS CHRIST

This is a book of prophecy that uncovers the testimony of Jesus to reveal and understand the message of God: to bring up the chronology of events that must take place before and during the millennium, which is the Day of the Lord. He will appear on earth for the second time to hold an iron of rod, to rule as Lord of lords and King of kings.

John, an apostle of Jesus Christ, was called by God in the Spirit at the Island of Patmos to write all that he witnessed as shown by God and to send a letter to the seven churches in Asia to tell them of God's message. Out of all the seven churches, only two were approved or blessed by God: the church of Smyrna, and the church of Philadelphia. They have the key of David, which opens the door of God's truth. These are the only two churches who both knew the Kenites (the offspring of Satan), who say that they are Jews but are from the synagogue of Satan, who claim that they are from the tribe of Judah, but lie and are now working for Satan to carry out his plan of deception to the whole world.

The original pages of the King James Bible are intact. All the pages in this book remain as they are. The author's pages are underneath, marked with "reminders" or "author's notes."

GOD'S MESSAGE TO THE SEVEN CHURCHES:

To understand God's message, we must get the truth by analysis using the four Ws:

> What: God's message: Corrections and warnings.
> Where: The message was received at the island of Patmos, then John was taken in spirit to see and write what he had observed.
> Who: Addressed to the seven churches.
> When: At the millennium (Day of the Lord).

THE SEVEN CHURCHES ARE:

(Author's notes continued)

1.   The Church of Ephesus: God named them the "Loveless Church." They started believing and loving God first, then they were deceived by the anti-Christ, where they found Baal worship or false teachings from false prophets. God is not happy with them. He expects you to love Him. He is a "jealous" God, your Creator. He made you for His pleasure (Revelation 4:11). You must repent, and for those who overcome, He will give you to eat from the Tree of Life. Our Lord Jesus Christ is the Tree of Life.

2.   The Church of Smyrna: This is a good or faithful church. They have the key of David to open the door of truth. They know their enemies (Kenites), and they are aware being sealed with God's truth in their minds. They will be protected from deceptions of Satan and the anti-Christ. Originally, God had shortened a seven-year tribulation to a fivemonth tribulation. They were to have a tribulation shortened to ten days individually, but for a nation, it would be two and a half months (twice), or five months instead of 7 years. Unless the Lord had shortened those days, no flesh will be saved; but for the elect's sake, whom He chose, He shortened those days (Mark 13:20).

3.   The Church of Pergamos: This is a corrupt Church. They also believe in Baal worship, which is idolatrous and false teachings. They were also told to repent.

4.   The Church of Thyatira: They also were snared with false teachings by false apostles, such as Jezebel, who claimed herself as a prophetess, misleading the servants of God and making them fall into sin by idolatry and fornication. They were told to repent.

5.   The Church of Sardis: Likewise, she is a corrupt Church that is teaching traditions of man, which is false worship. God warns them to watch because He is coming as a thief, meaning that you don't expect Him. They have already accepted the "fake" Christ, not looking for any other. They were deceived and were advised to repent.

6. The Church of Philadelphia: This is a faithful Church that God is happy with. They have the seal of God's truth in their minds that will always protect them from lies and deceptions of Satan. They possess the key of David, that is, they know the origin and seed-line generation of Jesus Christ, who is the truth. They are not like those false teachers who say they are Jews but are not and say they came from our brother Judah but belong to the synagogue of Satan who are teaching lies to mislead and to deceive.

7. The Church of Laodicea: This Church was warned to stay faithful and be a "doer" in serving God. They must have righteous acts to be clothed and not be exposed "naked" to feel shameful at judgment time. They were told to repent.

John, the scribe of the book of Revelation, was told to write to the seven churches to tell them God's messages and warnings that will come. The churches' faults and mistakes were identified and needed to be corrected because:

Through repentance, there is forgiveness.

"All sins will be forgiven, the sons of man, whatever blasphemes they may utter" (Mark 3:28-29).

The corrupt churches and unfaithful churches that were identified among the seven churches were holding the false teachings, such as the "fly-away doctrine" and warnings from the parables of tares:

"As the tares are gathered and burned in the fire, so it will be at the end of the age". (Matthew 13:36-40)

"Behold I am against your magic charms by which you hunt souls there like birds, I will tear them from your arms and let the souls go, the souls you hunt like birds". (Ezekiel 13:20)

It is not the name of the church that qualifies its name as the right church for worship, but it is rather the content of its message of whether or not they have the truth of God's words.

The key of David opens the door of truth that no one can close or open. It is the truth that the generation line of Jesus started from the creation of man in the garden of Eden from Adam and Eve to Abraham, to Isaac with the twelve tribes, to Noah's generation until King David, down to Mary and Joseph, Jesus' (flesh) parents on earth.

When they come to read the Bible, especially the book of Revelation, a lot of people usually get disappointed and develop a lack of interest and fear because they fail to understand the true message, thinking that the earth will be destroyed. No! On the contrary, (refer to Rev. chapter 22) God wants us to know about the future leading to a beautiful life in eternity! He loves us, especially those who follow His ways.

The Bible is a love letter to us (His children). Upon knowing His plans and teachings, we will be guided and achieve success and happiness in life. He wants us to know His truth and not be confused or deceived by false teachings, which are the lies that are taught by traditions of man (Colossians 2:8).

Satan and the anti-Christ group will spread misleading (false) doctrines that blind our minds. We must remain strong and wise and use the God-given wisdom of knowledge, which is the seal of truth in our minds, and upon believing and following His Word, His precious gift of eternal life will be achieved!

John was carried up in heaven in spirit and saw the throne of God. He saw the scene as described below:

1. God was sitting at the throne with a beautiful rainbow around the throne like an emerald.

2. The twenty-four elders were seated on their thrones around Him wearing golden crowns on their head and in white robes.

3. There were seven burning lamps, which are the seven spirits of God.

4. There was a sea of glass like crystal before the thrones.

5. Amid the throne and around were four living creatures full of eyes with six wings full of eyes around and within. Each had four faces. These are the chosen guards for the throne. They represented their groups in tribes with their identifying standards.

    a. The first living creature was like a lion—Judah represented the East.

    b. The second living creature was like a calf—Ephraim represented the West.

    c. The third living creature had a face like a man—Dan in the North.

    d. The fourth living creature was like a flying eagle—Reuben from the South.

They did not rest day or night giving glory and thanks to God. In the middle of all was seen a Lamb looking slain (Jesus was crucified). And God was on the throne holding a scroll in His right that was sealed with seals.

Following these are the seven seals, the seven trumps, and the seven vials to be watched and observed as they were unfolding the events or seasons, until Jesus Christ appears at the millennium to rule all nations, and then will follow the final judgment of our Father, the Godhead YHVH- Ya-ho-vah.

THE SEVEN SEALS
REVELATION CHAPTERS 6 & 7 (From the Bible)

6 I watched as the Lamb opened the first of the seven seals. Then I heard one of the four living creatures say in a voice like thunder, "Come!" 2 I looked, and there before me was a white horse! Its rider held a bow, and he was given a crown, and he rode out as a conqueror bent on conquest.

3 When the Lamb opened the second seal, I heard the second living creature say, "Come!" 4 Then another horse came out, a fiery red one. Its rider was given power to take peace from the earth and to make people kill each other. To him was given a large sword.

5 When the Lamb opened the third seal, I heard the third living creature say, "Come!" I looked, and there before me was a black horse! Its rider was holding a pair of scales in his hand. 6 Then I heard what sounded like a voice among the four living creatures, saying, "Two pounds of wheat for a day's wages, and six pounds of barley for a day's wages, and do not damage the oil and the wine!"

7 When the Lamb opened the fourth seal, I heard the voice of the fourth living creature say, "Come!" 8 I looked, and there before me was a pale horse! Its rider was named Death, and Hades was following close behind him. They were given power over a fourth of the earth to kill by sword, famine and plague, and by the wild beasts of the earth.

9 When he opened the fifth seal, I saw under the altar the souls of those who had been slain because of the word of God and the testimony they had maintained. 10 They called out in a loud voice, "How long, Sovereign Lord, holy and true, until you judge the inhabitants of the earth and avenge our blood?" 11 Then each of them was given

a white robe, and they were told to wait a little longer, until the full number of their fellow servants, their brothers and sisters who were killed just as they had been.

[12] I watched as he opened the sixth seal. There was a great earthquake. The sun turned black like sackcloth made of goat hair, the whole moon turned blood red, [13] and the stars in the sky fell to earth, as figs drop from a fig tree when shaken by a strong wind. [14] The heavens receded like a scroll being rolled up, and every mountain and island was removed from its place.

[15] Then the kings of the earth, the princes, the generals, the rich, the mighty, and everyone else, both slave and free, hid in caves and among the rocks of the mountains. [16] They called to the mountains and the rocks, "Fall on us and hide us[f] from the face of him who sits on the throne and from the wrath of the Lamb! [17] For the great day of their[g] wrath has come, and who can withstand it?"

7 After this I saw four angels standing at the four corners of the earth, holding back the four winds of the earth to prevent any wind from blowing on the land or on the sea or on any tree. [2] Then I saw another angel coming up from the east, having the seal of the living God. He called out in a loud voice to the four angels who had been given power to harm the land and the sea: [3] "Do not harm the land or the sea or the trees until we put a seal on the foreheads of the servants of our God."[4] Then I heard the number of those who were sealed: 144,000 from all the tribes of Israel.

[5] From the tribe of Judah 12,000 were sealed,
from the tribe of Reuben 12,000,
from the tribe of Gad 12,000,
[6] from the tribe of Asher 12,000,
from the tribe of Naphtali 12,000,
from the tribe of Manasseh 12,000,
[7] from the tribe of Simeon 12,000,
from the tribe of Levi 12,000,
from the tribe of Issachar 12,000,
[8] from the tribe of Zebulun 12,000,
from the tribe of Joseph 12,000,
from the tribe of Benjamin 12,000.

[9] After this I looked, and there before me was a great multitude that no one could count, from every nation, tribe, people and language, standing before the throne and before the Lamb. They were wearing white robes and were holding palm branches in their hands. [10] And they cried out in a loud voice:

"Salvation belongs to our God, who sits on the throne, and to the Lamb." 11 All the angels were standing around the throne and around the elders and the four living creatures. They fell down on their faces before the throne and worshiped God, 12 saying: "Amen! Praise and glory and wisdom and thanks and honor and power and strength be to our God for ever and ever. Amen!"

¹³ Then one of the elders asked me, "These in white robes—who are they, and where did they come from?" ¹⁴ I answered, "Sir, you know." And he said, "These are they who have come out of the great tribulation; they have washed their robes and made them white in the blood of the Lamb. ¹⁵ Therefore, "they are before the throne of God and serve him day and night in his temple; and he who sits on the throne will shelter them with his presence. ¹⁶ 'Never again will they hunger; never again will they thirst. The sun will not beat down on them,' nor any scorching heat. ¹⁷ For the Lamb at the center of the throne will be their shepherd; 'he will lead them to springs of living water.' 'And God will wipe away every tear from their eyes.'"

AUTHOR'S NOTES:

Seals are the knowledge of the truth of God so that we are not deceived by the repulsive lies of Satan and the anti-Christ to fall away from God.

The plagues to happen are contained in each seal and are to take place as laid out. No one could open them, but Jesus Christ, who prevailed to open the seals one at a time.

1. The first seal was opened, and a white horse was seen, and the rider was wearing a cheap fabric imitation and was given a bow and a crown on his head and went out conquering. This is the false Christ who comes first on earth to deceive the whole world with a flood of lies; teaching falsehoods to mislead and confuse people to do all possibilities to worship him. He always wants to be ahead of Jesus Christ.

2. The second seal is a fiery red horse, seen with the rider with a sword to take peace from earth. People will be killing one another.

3. The third seal is a black horse with a rider holding a pair of scales. This could be a symbol of inflation or a strike of food scarcity.

4. Then the fourth seal was opened, and a pale horse was seen. The name of the rider was Death, and Hades followed him. These were given the power over a fourth of the earth to kill with sword, hunger, and death by the beasts of the earth. With God's seal on our forehead and with the gospel armor of God that we wear (Ephesians 6:14-17), we have the weapons to overcome Satan's deception.

"Stand therefore, having girded yourself with truth, having put on the breast plate of righteousness, and having shod your feet with the preparation with the gospel of peace; above all, taking the shield of faith with which you will be able to quench all the fiery darts of the

wicked one and take the helmet of salvation and the sword of the spirit which is the word of God". (Ephesians 6:14)

We were given authority by Jesus Christ over all our enemies using Jesus Christ's name (Luke 10:19).

5.   When the fifth seal was opened, the altar of God was seen, with the souls of those servants of God who were killed because of their testimony against the enemy when they were delivered up to them. They asked, "How long, O God, will you judge and avenge us upon those who dwell on earth?" They were given white robes and told to wait for a little season until the number of those who were killed, as they were, was to be completed. It is important to notice that at the fifth seal, the gospel of God must be preached in all the world first to make known the importance of God's message, so that they will wake up to the truth before the anti-Christ arrives.

*6.   At the opening of the sixth seal, there was a great earthquake and darkening upon the earth. The sun became black and the moon became like blood, the sky receded, and every mountain and island were displaced. This dimming light is caused by the coming of Satan and the anti-Christ. Satan and his angels had war with Michael and his army. They were defeated. Satan was angry, realizing that he only had a short time of five months. He comes to deceive the whole world by persecuting and going after God's children. We must keep the seal of God in our minds and not be deceived! For those who are not educated with God's Word, they will need to learn and know the enemy to avoid deception. God warned us, saying, "I have foretold you all things" (Mark 13:23). Jesus also wants us to learn the parable of the fig tree (Matthew 24:32), which depicts the harvest of the earth. We must be aware of the chronological order of events happening during the time or seasons of the seals, trumpets, and vials, because Jesus told us that all prophecies would be fulfilled. We were told to observe and watch the signs leading to the close of the age, for His words will not fail. Deceived men with false teachings prayed that the rocks of the mountains would fall upon them, causing them to even seek death, but death will flee from them. They have realized they already accepted and were worshipping the false Jesus Christ and now are so ashamed to face the true Jesus.

*7.   There was silence in heaven for one half hour to watch and observe the earth (equivalent to two and a half months on earth). Satan was on earth and started persecuting the people of God by revealing tricks and miracles to convince and make us fall away from God. He snaps his fingers to create fire and lighting coming from heaven. He will play the role of Jesus Christ, and he comes peacefully and prosperously (no violence or bloodshed, gun shooting, or nuclear bombing). He plays the role as the "savior" of the world. (Daniel 11:20-27) Satan and his supporters will use massive lies to confuse, mislead, and deceive people with false teachings and doctrines like the "rapture theory." At the four corners of the earth, there were four wicked angels (Satan's) to harm the earth and the sea. They were told by an angel of God not to harm the trees, earth, and the sea until the one hundred forty-four thousand servants of God from among the twelve tribes of the children of Israel were sealed. Twelve thousand from each tribe (144,000 in total) were sealed (Revelation 7:5-8): Tribe of Judah, Ruben, Gad, Asher, Nephthali, Manasseh, Simeon, Levi, Issachar, Zebulun, Joseph, and Benjamin.

THE SEVEN TRUMPS
REVELATION CHAPTER 8 (From the Bible)

8 When he opened the seventh seal, there was silence in heaven for about half an hour. (2 ½ months x 2 = 5 months on earth or 1 hour in heaven).

[2] And I saw the seven angels who stand before God, and seven trumpets were given to them.

[3] Another angel, who had a golden censer, came and stood at the altar. He was given much incense to offer, with the prayers of all God's people, on the golden altar in front of the throne. [4] The smoke of the incense, together with the prayers of God's people, went up before God from the angel's hand. [5] Then the angel took the censer, filled it with fire from the altar, and hurled it on the earth; and there came peals of thunder, rumblings, flashes of lightning and an earthquake.

[6] Then the seven angels who had the seven trumpets prepared to sound them.

[7] The first angel sounded his trumpet, and there came hail and fire mixed with blood, and it was hurled down on the earth. A third of the earth was burned up, a third of the trees were burned up, and all the green grass was burned up.

[8] The second angel sounded his trumpet, and something like a huge mountain, all ablaze, was thrown into the sea. A third of the sea turned into blood, [9] a third of the living creatures in the sea died, and a third of the ships were destroyed.

[10] The third angel sounded his trumpet, and a great star, blazing like a torch, fell from the sky on a third of the rivers and on the springs of water— [11] the name of the star is Wormwood. A third of the waters turned bitter, and many people died from the waters that had become bitter.

¹² The fourth angel sounded his trumpet, and a third of the sun was struck, a third of the moon, and a third of the stars, so that a third of them turned dark. A third of the day was without light, and also a third of the night.

¹³ As I watched, I heard an eagle that was flying in midair call out in a loud voice: "Woe! Woe! Woe to the inhabitants of the earth, because of the trumpet blasts about to be sounded by the other three angels!"

When Jesus opened the seventh seal, there was silence in heaven for half an hour, equivalent to two and a half months (there was peace in heaven for Satan, and his fallen angels were cast out to earth). This period indicates that heaven is observing what is going on with the earth, for Satan was defeated.

Trumpets are symbols for executions of actions. Seven angels of God were given the seven trumpets: another angel with a censer placed much incense for the prayers of the saints who were before the throne and made it ascend to the throne of God:

AUTHOR'S NOTES:

The trumps are the execution of God's command. It is always onethird of the people killed because Satan caused the rebellion in the first earth age in which a third of God's angels were deceived, which caused the *katabole*.

I.   The first trumpet sounded, and hail and fire were thrown to the earth. A third of the trees and green grass were burned.

II. The second trumpet sounded, and something like a great mountain burning with fire was thrown into the sea. A third of the sea (people) died, and a third of the living creatures in the sea were killed, and a third of the ships were destroyed. It happened with the Tyrus commerce, which was in an island that held all the goodly precious commerce of different nations in the old times.

The following prediction proved it:

"Your riches, wears and merchandise, your mariners and pilots, your caulkers and merchandisers, all your men of war who are in you and the entire company, which is in your midst, will fall into the midst of the seas on the day of your ruin" (Ezekiel 27:37).

III. A great star fell from heaven like a burning torch and fell on a third of the rivers and on the spring of waters. The name of the star is Wormwood. Many men died due to the bitterness of water.

IV. The fourth trumpet was sounded. A third of the sun, a third of the moon, and a third of the stars were struck and darkened the earth. There was an angel flying through the midst of heaven announcing about three woes on earth (bad events coming).

Those with the seal of God will be able to escape from the hour of temptation of Satan (five months). If you are standing firm on the Rock (Jesus Christ), you will not be affected by the plague. You will be protected from Satan's wickedness because you are sealed with God's truth.

REVELATION CHAPTER 9
(From the Bible)

9 The fifth angel sounded his trumpet, and I saw a star that had fallen from the sky to the earth. The star was given the key to the shaft of the Abyss. ² When he opened the Abyss, smoke rose from it like the smoke from a gigantic furnace. The sun and sky were darkened by the smoke from the Abyss. ³ And out of the smoke locusts came down on the earth and were given power like that of scorpions of the earth. ⁴ They were told not to harm the grass of the earth or any plant or tree, but only those people who did not have the seal of God on their foreheads. ⁵ They were not allowed to kill them but only to torture them for five months. And the agony they suffered was like that of the sting of a scorpion when it strikes. ⁶ During those days people will seek death but will not find it; they will long to die, but death will elude them.

⁷ The locusts looked like horses prepared for battle. On their heads they wore something like crowns of gold, and their faces resembled human faces. ⁸ Their hair was like women's hair, and their teeth were like lions' teeth. ⁹ They had breastplates like breastplates of iron, and the sound of their wings was like the thundering of many horses and chariots rushing into battle. ¹⁰ They had tails with stingers, like scorpions, and in their tails they had power to torment people for five months. ¹¹ They had as king over them the angel of the Abyss, whose name in Hebrew is Abaddon and in Greek is Apollyon (both names mean Destroyer).

¹² The first woe is past; two other woes are yet to come.

¹³ The sixth angel sounded his trumpet, and I heard a voice coming from the four horns of the golden altar that is before God. ¹⁴ It said to the sixth angel who had the trumpet, "Release the four angels who are bound at the great river Euphrates." ¹⁵ And the four angels who had been kept ready for this very hour and day and month and year were

released to kill a third of mankind. [16] The number of the mounted troops was twice ten thousand times ten thousand. I heard their number.

[17] The horses and riders I saw in my vision looked like this: Their breastplates were fiery red, dark blue, and yellow as sulfur. The heads of the horses resembled the heads of lions, and out of their mouths came fire, smoke and sulfur. [18] A third of mankind was killed by the three plagues of fire, smoke and sulfur that came out of their mouths. [19] The power of the horses was in their mouths and in their tails; for their tails were like snakes, having heads with which they inflict injury.

[20] The rest of mankind who were not killed by these plagues still did not repent of the work of their hands; they did not stop worshiping demons, and idols of gold, silver, bronze, stone and wood—idols that cannot see or hear or walk. [21] Nor did they repent of their murders, their magic arts, their sexual immorality or their thefts.

AUTHOR'S NOTES

V.   At the sound of the fifth trumpet, an angel was given the key to the bottomless pit. He opened it, and a great smoke rose like that coming from a great furnace, and there was darkening because of the smoke in the pit (God used locusts as an analogy to describe the enemy). Then locusts came out upon the earth: these are the Kenites (offspring of Satan). To them was given the power like the power of a scorpion when they attack. They have two powerful pinchers in their mouth to bite the skin, and they use the tail to sting with the pincher to inject poison to paralyze the victim until he is gone. This is Satan's method of attacking his victim by injecting deception into the minds until the person gives up and will worship him. The enemy is allowed to torment men who were not sealed of God's truth, but he is not allowed to kill them for five months. Because of the torments, men will seek death but will not find it.

The five-month cycle of locusts will prevail. The locusts have a king over them, who is identified as Satan—the king of the bottomless pit:

a.   Abaddon—Satan's name in Hebrew.
b.   Apollyon (Apollya - female)—Satan's name in Greek

Both names mean "destroyer." These are the armies of Satan that work with false apostles to teach lies, traditions of men, that deceive and mislead people to confusion.

VI.   The sixth trumpet sounded. There were four bound angels (wicked angels) at the River Euphrates who were released for the hour and day and month and year to kill a third of mankind instantly.

The number of the enemy is so great; it is two hundred million. Their weapons coming from their mouths are smoke, fire, and brimstone. They are using massive lies teaching falsehoods that will hurt if you allow them. They teach idolatry, which is worship of idols or images of gold, silver, brass, stone, and wood. They committed sins of murder, sexual immorality, sorceries, and theft. The rest of mankind that were not killed still did not repent of their evil deeds.

VII. The 7th Trump is on Page 82.

REVELATION CHAPTER 10
(From the Bible)

10 Then I saw another mighty angel coming down from heaven. He was robed in a cloud, with a rainbow above his head; his face was like the sun, and his legs were like fiery pillars. [2] He was holding a little scroll, which lay open in his hand. He planted his right foot on the sea and his left foot on the land, [3] and he gave a loud shout like the roar of a lion. When he shouted, the voices of the seven thunders spoke. [4] And when the seven thunders spoke, I was about to write; but I heard a voice from heaven say, "Seal up what the seven thunders have said and do not write it down."

[5] Then the angel I had seen standing on the sea and on the land raised his right hand to heaven. [6] And he swore by Him who lives for ever and ever, who created the heavens and all that is in them, the earth and all that is in it, and the sea and all that is in it, and said, "There will be no more delay! [7] But in the days when the seventh angel is about to sound his trumpet, the mystery of God will be accomplished, just as he announced to his servants the prophets."

[8] Then the voice that I had heard from heaven spoke to me once more: "Go, take the scroll that lies open in the hand of the angel who is standing on the sea and on the land."

[9] So I went to the angel and asked him to give me the little scroll. He said to me, "Take it and eat it. It will turn your stomach sour, but 'in your mouth it will be as sweet as honey.'" [10] I took the little scroll from the angel's hand and ate it. It tasted as sweet as honey in my mouth, but when I had eaten it, my stomach turned sour. [11] Then I was told, "You must prophesy again about many peoples, nations, languages and kings."

AUTHOR'S NOTES:

An angel of God had the little book (Bible) in his hand, and a loud voice of seven thunders sounded:

John: I was about to write but a voice from heaven prevented me. *"Seal up, do not write."* The mystery of God would be finished because He had already declared it to His servants, the prophets. In the book of Amos, it states:

> *"Surely the Lord God does nothing, unless He reveals His secret to His servants the prophets". (Amos 3:7)*

The voice from heaven told me, "Go take the little book. Take and eat it, it will make your stomach bitter, but it will be as sweet as honey in your mouth." And I took the little book out of the angel's hand and ate it. I did as I was told, and when I ate the words of God, it tasted so sweet and pure, but when I taught the words of God to men, there were controversies, ridicules, different comments, and disagreements that would make my stomach bitter.

To prophesy or teach God's Word to peoples, nations, tongues, and kings was commanded to me.

We who have the knowledge of God are supposed to teach so as to make people learn the truth and wake up from deception and see reality.

REVELATION CHAPTER **11**
(From the Bible)

11 I was given a reed like a measuring rod and was told, "Go and measure the temple of God and the altar, with its worshipers. ² But exclude the outer court; do not measure it, because it has been given to the Gentiles. They will trample on the holy city for 42 months. ³ And I will appoint my two witnesses, and they will prophesy for 1,260 days, clothed in sackcloth." ⁴ They are "the two olive trees" and the two lampstands, and "they stand before the Lord of the earth." ⁵ If anyone tries to harm them, fire comes from their mouths and devours their enemies. This is how anyone who wants to harm them must die. ⁶ They have power to shut up the heavens so that it will not rain during the time they are prophesying; and they have power to turn the waters into blood and to strike the earth with every kind of plague as often as they want.

⁷ Now when they have finished their testimony, the beast that comes up from the Abyss will attack them and overpower and kill them. ⁸ Their bodies will lie in the public square of the great city—which is figuratively called Sodom and Egypt—where also their Lord was crucified. ⁹ For three and a half days some from every people, tribe, language and nation will gaze on their bodies and refuse them burial. ¹⁰ The inhabitants of the earth will gloat over them and will celebrate by sending each other gifts, because these two prophets had tormented those who live on the earth.

¹¹ But after the three and a half days the breath of life from God entered them, and they stood on their feet, and terror struck those who saw them. ¹² Then they heard a loud voice from heaven saying to them, "Come up here." And they went up to heaven in a cloud, while their enemies looked on.

13 At that very hour there was a severe earthquake and a tenth of the city collapsed. Seven thousand people were killed in the earthquake, and the survivors were terrified and gave glory to the God of heaven.

14 The second woe has passed; the third woe is coming soon.

15 The seventh angel sounded his trumpet, and there were loud voices in heaven, which said:

"The kingdom of the world has become the kingdom of our Lord and of his Messiah, and he will reign for ever and ever."

16 And the twenty-four elders, who were seated on their thrones before God, fell on their faces and worshiped God, 17 saying: B"We give thanks to you, Lord God Almighty, the One who is and who was, because you have taken your great power and have begun to reign.

18 The nations were angry, and your wrath has come. The time has come for judging the dead, and for rewarding your servants the prophets and your people who revere your name, both great and small— and for destroying those who destroy the earth."

19 Then God's temple in heaven was opened, and within his temple was seen the ark of his covenant. And there came flashes of lightning, rumblings, peals of thunder, an earthquake and a severe hailstorm.

NOTES FOR REVELATION CHAPTER 11:

The Gentiles from the city were exposed to false worship and doctrines, which led them to believe the false prophets. Deception of the enemy was so intense, and God sent His two witnesses to prophesy (Elijah and Moses) for one thousand two hundred sixty days (three and a half years), about ten days before Satan and the anti-Christ appear, and the two witnesses were given mighty power against the enemy. If anyone tries to harm them, fire proceeds from their mouth and devours their enemies. This method of killing is their weapon that comes from God. They were given a tremendous power over the wicked people to strike with plagues.

In the old times, when the prophet Elijah prayed earnestly that it would not rain, it did not rain on the land for three and a half years, and then he prayed again, and heaven opened and gave rain over the earth, which produced its fruits (1 Kings 18:1-42). With God's blessing, Elijah's prayers were answered.

> *"Behold, I will send you Elijah, the prophet before the coming of the great and dreadful Day of the Lord"(Malachi 4:5).*

With Moses, during Israel's time of slavery in Egypt, he did a lot of service for God in bringing plagues upon the land Egypt to help free the children of God from the rule of Pharaoh's oppression.

These two servants of God were sent, with the great power of the Holy Spirit, to help during those evil and dark times. The menorah, which is the seven-stemmed candle holder, contained the oil (symbolic of the presence of the Holy Spirit) that was continuously feeding oil to keep it lit for the seven thousand elects of God, who were around the dark world of Satan. After their testimony, the beast, who is Satan, fought against the two witnesses and killed them. God allowed this to happen to prove that He is the God who conquers death.

God's strict order was not to harm His elect: "Do not harm My elect" (Revelation 9:4). Satan disobeyed God while the deceived people rejoiced that the two (Elijah and Moses) witnesses were killed. They did not allow their dead bodies to be put in graves but let them be displayed for observation in the arena of Jerusalem. They wanted to see if their bodies would resurrect. After three and a half days of exposure to all peoples, tribes, races, and nations, they saw the two dead bodies start to move, stand, and walk. Great fear came upon those observers with a strong paralyzing fear. God made life enter their dead bodies again. A voice from heaven was heard, "Come up here." They saw them go up in the clouds. Then there was a great earthquake and noises and bright lighting around. Satan, including the seven thousand fallen angels, were killed. At the same time, the seven thousand elects were saved and gave glory to God (Revelation 9:5).

VII.   And the seventh trumpet sounded, and at an instant, everyone was changed into a new world dimension (into spirits). Jesus appeared!

"In the twinkling of an eye, at the last trumpet. For the trump will sound and the dead will be raised incorruptible and we shall all be changed" (1 Corinthians 15:52).

Every knee shall bow when they see Jesus, because Jesus has come! This is the age of the millennium, the Day of the Lord (Isaiah 45:23)!

REVELATION CHAPTER 12
(From the Bible)

12 A great sign appeared in heaven: a woman clothed with the sun, with the moon under her feet and a crown of twelve stars on her head. [2] She was pregnant and cried out in pain as she was about to give birth. [3] Then another sign appeared in heaven: an enormous red dragon with seven heads and ten horns and seven crowns on its heads. [4] Its tail swept a third of the stars out of the sky and flung them to the earth. The dragon stood in front of the woman who was about to give birth, so that it might devour her child the moment he was born. [5] She gave birth to a son, a male child, who "will rule all the nations with an iron scepter." And her child was snatched up to God and to his throne. [6] The woman fled into the wilderness to a place prepared for her by God, where she might be taken care of for 1,260 days.

[7] Then war broke out in heaven. Michael and his angels fought against the dragon, and the dragon and his angels fought back. [8] But he was not strong enough, and they lost their place in heaven. [9] The great dragon was hurled down—that ancient serpent called the devil, or Satan, who leads the whole world astray. He was hurled to the earth, and his angels with him.

[10] Then I heard a loud voice in heaven say: "Now have come the salvation and the power and the kingdom of our God, and the authority of his Messiah. For the accuser of our brothers and sisters, who accuses them before our God day and night, has been hurled down. [11] They triumphed over him by the blood of the Lamb and by the word of their testimony; they did not love their lives so much as to shrink from death. [12] Therefore rejoice, you heavens and you who dwell in them! But woe to the earth and the sea, because the devil has gone down to you! He is filled with fury, because he knows that his time is short."

¹³ When the dragon saw that he had been hurled to the earth, he pursued the woman who had given birth to the male child. ¹⁴ The woman was given the two wings of a great eagle, so that she might fly to the place prepared for her in the wilderness, where she would be taken care of for a time, times and half a time, out of the serpent's reach. ¹⁵ Then from his mouth the serpent spewed water like a river, to overtake the woman and sweep her away with the torrent. ¹⁶ But the earth helped the woman by opening its mouth and swallowing the river that the dragon had spewed out of his mouth. ¹⁷ Then the dragon was enraged at the woman and went off to wage war against the rest of her offspring—those who keep God's commands and hold fast their testimony about Jesus.

AUTHOR'S NOTE:

Mother Israel was that nation mentioned in the Bible who has the twelve garlands of stars on her head. She bore a Child (Jesus) that was caught up to God and His throne to rule all nations with a rod of iron.

Satan was that dragon (cast out with his fallen angels to earth), also called the devil. He went to persecute the woman with his tremendous flood of lies to deceive. But the woman fled into the wilderness, where she belongs, as planned by God for three and a half years. Satan went to make war with the rest of her offspring who keep the commandments of God and have the testimony of Jesus. As Satan caused the *katabole* rebellion with his seven thousand fallen angels, it caused the destruction of the first earth age. And then later, they fought again with Michael in a war in heaven and Satan lost. The wicked angels were finally thrown down to earth, as they did not have a place anymore in heaven. They are already destined to be killed at the coming back of Jesus Christ (Jude 6).

This is the time when he started his role as the false Christ throughout the world. He started to commit his evil deeds by going after the children of God on earth with his intensive lies by teaching false doctrines and using words with flattery, miracles of snapping his fingers to cause fire or lightning to fall down from the sky to convince people on earth of his authority.

The unlearned do not know the difference between the false and the true Christ. They are easily convinced to fall for his wise tricks. But those with the seal of God's truth will find him an abomination. This is the reason why God wrote His message of warnings to let us know His truth so we do not fall into Satan's camp. They have strong faith and firm conviction, being sealed with the truth, and they are always protected by God. Satan and the anti-Christ have no power over them.

With the flood of lies that Satan used to tempt the people on earth, God always knows how to protect His own. He says, *"I will never leave you or forsake you"* (Hebrew 13:5).

The earth is a creation of God that helps people understand as they learn of God's many blessings.

REVELATION CHAPTER 13
(From the Bible)

13 The dragon stood on the shore of the sea. And I saw a beast coming out of the sea. It had ten horns and seven heads, with ten crowns on its horns, and on each head a blasphemous name. ² The beast I saw resembled a leopard but had feet like those of a bear and a mouth like that of a lion. The dragon gave the beast his power and his throne and great authority. ³ One of the heads of the beast seemed to have had a fatal wound, but the fatal wound had been healed. The whole world was filled with wonder and followed the beast. ⁴ People worshiped the dragon because he had given authority to the beast, and they also worshiped the beast and asked, "Who is like the beast? Who can wage war against it?"

⁵ The beast was given a mouth to utter proud words and blasphemies and to exercise its authority for forty-two months. ⁶ It opened its mouth to blaspheme God, and to slander his name and his dwelling place and those who live in heaven. ⁷ It was given power to wage war against God's holy people and to conquer them. And it was given authority over every tribe, people, language and nation. ⁸ All inhabitants of the earth will worship the beast—all whose names have not been written in the Lamb's book of life, the Lamb who was slain from the creation of the world.

⁹ Whoever has ears, let them hear.

¹⁰ "If anyone is to go into captivity, into captivity they will go.

If anyone is to be killed with the sword, with the sword they will be killed."

This calls for patient endurance and faithfulness on the part of God's people.

¹¹ Then I saw a second beast, coming out of the earth. It had two horns like a lamb, but it spoke like a dragon. ¹² It exercised all the authority of the first beast on its behalf and

made the earth and its inhabitants worship the first beast, whose fatal wound had been healed. [13] And it performed great signs, even causing fire to come down from heaven to the earth in full view of the people. [14] Because of the signs it was given power to perform on behalf of the first beast, it deceived the inhabitants of the earth. It ordered them to set up an image in honor of the beast who was wounded by the sword and yet lived. [15] The second beast was given power to give breath to the image of the first beast, so that the image could speak and cause all who refused to worship the image to be killed. [16] It also forced all people, great and small, rich and poor, free and slave, to receive a mark on their right hands or on their foreheads [their minds or their brain], so that they could not buy or sell unless they had the mark, which is the name of the beast or the number of its name.

[18] This calls for wisdom. Let the person who has insight calculate the number of the beast, for it is the number of a man. That number is 666.

AUTHOR'S NOTE:

The beast rising out of the sea with seven heads and ten horns on his head with a blasphemous name written is the anti-Christ.

The dragon is Satan, who gave his power, throne, and authority to the beast, which caused the one world system, a multi-headed governmental\ system. With "oneness of minds" and ways among nations, this one world system will cause broken peace. However, it created the deadly wound (temporary peace among nations), but it was revived by Satan. He became the leader of it.

The one world system was granted to continue for forty-two months. He made war with the saints and was given power to overcome the saints. God, through the Holy Spirit, worked with the elect. When they are delivered up to testify against the enemy, they will speak what is given them in that hour and allow the Holy Spirit to speak through them, and everyone will hear His words. The sword of God is His tongue that has two sharp edges that cuts lies and falsehoods and brings out the truth. The Holy Spirit's cloven tongue speaks with all kinds of dialects and languages of the nations at one time and all will understand.

REMINDER:

What is "on your forehead" is in your brain. The mind must be aware of the truth of God and the mark on the right hand means you would not work for Satan's false teachings or doctrines. All prophecies that concern moons are about Satan's evil prophecy that indicates the night, while prophecy about days indicates the time for the children of God because we are children of the Light.

The false prophets, with their false doctrines, led to the teachings of traditions of man that voids the Word of God. These false teachings are what cause many people to be confused and deceived.

Satan was on earth playing the role of Jesus Christ. This is blasphemy. He looked like the slain lamb but spoke like a dragon. He always wanted to copy Jesus with impressive tricks to deceive the world. He is coming peacefully and prosperously. He performs great miracles, such as snapping his fingers to create fire or lightning in the sight of the beast, and in the sight of man, to impress and to be worshipped. He plays the role of Jesus as a savior. That is why no one can say he could harm anyone physically, nor would bring violence or killings with the use of vicious weapons. He will use the power of his mouth with hot lies—a flood of lies. With that method, he will use his false prophets to teach false doctrines like the "rapture theory" that says, "I come to fly you away to save your souls" (Ezekiel 13:20).

He will tell the people who are not learned about God to make an image to speak and to receive his mark on their forehead (in their minds). And in their right hand (to work), with Satan's evil deeds, so that those who would not worship him will be killed. Furthermore, he tells people that no one may buy or sell except those who have his mark of his name and his number of 666.

The use of the image of the beast is tantamount to the use of television sets to preach all around the world of today! At the same time, the truth of God can also be taught. We must be careful not to be fully involved, so we do not get caught up with their clandestine shows of entertainment, which might carry us away from God.

There are two tribulations coming:

1. Satan's tribulation—These are the sequences of events that will happen as mentioned in the seven seals, seven trumpets, and seven vials. These are destructive, bitter, and painful. This is the reason why Jesus Christ has shortened the tribulation of Satan to five months from seven years for the elects' sake, or no flesh will be able to live (Matthew 24:32). Individually, it is a ten-day trial (Revelation 2:10); for the nations, it is five months (Matthew 24:22).

2. God's tribulation—God's tribulations are not meant for His followers. They have the seal of knowledge of God in their minds that protects them. Satan has no power over them. The just and faithful (elect) were given authority and power over all their enemies, and nothing by any means will hurt them (Luke 10:19).

The one world system (multi-headed government system) will prevail at the end times. Satan will use the four hidden dynasties to trouble the world:

a. Political/Governmental—The different laws and rules of government will be disregarded. Lawlessness will abound.

b. Financial—Problems of financial manipulations will exist (e.g.: increase in taxes, identity theft, Increased capitalism, usury, etc.).

c. Educational—Students become violent, fighting one another in streets, increased protesting, professors infiltrate educational teachings with false prophecies, and educational standards become low. It is sad to note that since the schools have eliminated sessions of prayers in classes, or a total ban from students and parents, it also became an absolute disregard of faith in God.

d.   Religious—Satan and the anti-Christ will spread false teachings that will brainwash people with lies. Teaching traditions of man voids the Word of God (Ephesians 5:6). Let no one deceive you with empty words.

Beware lest anyone cheat you through philosophy and empty deceit, according to traditions of man, according to the basic principle of the world, and not according to Christ. (Colossians 2:8)

God stated:

"Behold, I am against your charms by which you hunt souls like birds: You saw kerchiefs and pillow cases to cover my knuckles and hands to save souls. I will tear them from your arms and let the souls go, the souls you hunt like birds. I am against it!" (Ezekiel 13:20)

Satan will say I come to fly you away to save your souls. But God says there is no other way to save souls and have salvation except through Jesus Christ, the truth. This statement of Satan is convincing and will easily fool people and cause them to fall into his trap.

There are two tribulations:

1.   Satan's tribulation—He will give power to the false prophets to teach or preach traditions of falsehoods, such as the rapture theory or the "fly away" doctrine (Ezekiel 13:20).

Satan will insist on the issue of the mark of the beast—a mark on their foreheads—which is on their mind to worship him. They will also receive a mark on their right hand that allows them to work for their corrupt church. No one may buy or sell except those who have the mark and name of the beast, or they will be killed. According to God, we who are sealed with the truth will have ten days of trial to endure, but for the nations, it will be five months, which has been shortened from seven years by God for our sake. God really knows how to take care of His own people. As He said, He will never leave us, or never forsake us (Hebrew 13:5).

2.   God's tribulation—His cup of wrath that is poured out in successive events upon all who offend at the end of time due to disobedience, sins, perversion, and other ways of wickedness. However, we, as believers, are not supposed to be affected by His wrath because we have the seal of God. We are protected by Him. The wrath is not meant for us, but for the enemies.

REVELATION CHAPTER **14**
(From the Bible)

14 Then I looked, and there before me was the Lamb, standing on Mount Zion, and with him 144,000 who had his name and his Father's name written on their foreheads. [2] And I heard a sound from heaven like the roar of rushing waters and like a loud peal of thunder. The sound I heard was like that of harpists playing their harps. [3] And they sang a new song before the throne and before the four living creatures and the elders. No one could learn the song except the 144,000 who had been redeemed from the earth. [4] These are those who did not defile themselves with women, for they remained virgins. They follow the Lamb wherever he goes. They were purchased from among mankind and offered as first fruits to God and the Lamb. [5] No lie was found in their mouths; they are blameless.

[6] Then I saw another angel flying in midair, and he had the eternal gospel to proclaim to those who live on the earth—to every nation, tribe, language and people. [7] He said in a loud voice, "Fear God and give him glory, because the hour of his judgment has come. Worship him who made the heavens, the earth, the sea and the springs of water."

[8] A second angel followed and said, "'Fallen! Fallen is Babylon the Great,' which made all the nations drink the maddening wine of her adulteries."

[9] A third angel followed them and said in a loud voice: "If anyone worships the beast and its image and receives its mark on their forehead or on their hand, [10] they, too, will drink the wine of God's fury, which has been poured full strength into the cup of his wrath. They will be tormented with burning sulfur in the presence of the holy angels and of the Lamb. [11] And the smoke of their torment will rise for ever and ever. There will be no rest day or night for those who worship the beast and its image, or for

anyone who receives the mark of its name." ¹² This calls for patient endurance on the part of the people of God who keep his commands and remain faithful to Jesus.

¹³ Then I heard a voice from heaven say, "Write this: Blessed are the dead who die in the Lord from now on."

"Yes," says the Spirit, "they will rest from their labor, for their deeds will follow them."

¹⁴ I looked, and there before me was a white cloud, and seated on the cloud was one like a son of man[b] with a crown of gold on his head and a sharp sickle in his hand. ¹⁵ Then another angel came out of the temple and called in a loud voice to him who was sitting on the cloud, "Take your sickle and reap, because the time to reap has come, for the harvest of the earth is ripe." ¹⁶ So he who was seated on the cloud swung his sickle over the earth, and the earth was harvested.

¹⁷ Another angel came out of the temple in heaven, and he too had a sharp sickle. ¹⁸ Still another angel, who had charge of the fire, came from the altar and called in a loud voice to him who had the sharp sickle, "Take your sharp sickle and gather the clusters of grapes from the earth's vine, because its grapes are ripe." ¹⁹ The angel swung his sickle on the earth, gathered its grapes and threw them into the great winepress of God's wrath. ²⁰ They were trampled in the winepress outside the city, and blood flowed out of the press, rising as high as the horses' bridles for a distance of 1,600 stadia.

AUTHOR'S NOTES:

This fourteenth chapter was written about the earth.

There were one hundred forty-four thousand people who were sealed with the truth of God. At first, they were not serious with their faith, because they were disarrayed and were misled for a while. However, they were redeemed with the truth by the elect who were called the "Zadok" (priests) or teachers. They overcame the misleading doctrines of Satan. Now, they stand firm on the "Rock," who is our Lord, Jesus Christ. The seven thousand elects from the very first world age, and the one hundred forty-four thousand sealed, are always guided, led, and protected by God.

An angel with the gospel of truth came out of heaven and began to preach and warn the people, races, multitudes, and tongues about the coming wrath of God at the end times. Anyone who received the mark of the beast on his forehead and on his hand will be judged by Almighty God. He will be tormented with fire, smoke, and brimstone day and night with no rest in the presence of the holy angels and the Lamb.

This warning follows this saying, "Blessed are the dead who die in the Lord that they rest from their labors and their works follow them" (Revelation 14:13).

When we die, the only thing we can take with us is our works and merits, or what we have done on earth.

The works are made up of fine linen, which are the righteous acts that will be used to judge the person at the white throne judgment (Revelation 20:13).

One like the Son of Man sitting on a cloud, having a golden crown on his head and a sharp sickle in His hand, was told by an angel to reap the earth for the grapes that were fully ripe (people). Jesus and His angels reaped the grapevine, as it is harvest time.

A sharp sickle in agriculture is used for harvesting any type of grain, such as wheat or barley. One angel after the other came out to announce about the harvest of the earth. Harvest time is the end times.

"Their vine is not our vine." The vine of Satan are those people on earth who were hooked to his doctrine of lies and traditions of man, which are false philosophies that are confusing and misleading. Their rock (Satan), is not our "Rock" (Jesus). The vine of Satan is the main target. God is angry at his growing falsehood.

The sixth angel, who has the power over fire, reaped and gathered "clusters of grapes" and threw them at the winepress of the wrath of God, outside the city, and blood came out, up to the horse's bridle for one thousand six hundred furlongs (about 180—200 miles).

This type of harvest is for those who do not believe God and for those disobedient to His words. But, for those who are learned of His commandments and teachings are protected, as He says, "I will never forsake you, I will never leave you" (Hebrew 13:5).

Revelation Chapter 15
(From the Bible)

15 I saw in heaven another great and marvelous sign: seven angels with the seven last plagues—last, because with them God's wrath is completed. ² And I saw what looked like a sea of glass glowing with fire and, standing beside the sea, those who had been victorious over the beast and its image and over the number of its name. They held harps given them by God ³ and sang the song of God's servant Moses and of the Lamb:

"Great and marvelous are your deeds, Lord God Almighty. Just and true are your ways, King of the nations. ⁴ Who will not fear you, Lord, and bring glory to your name? For you alone are holy. All nations will come and worship before you, for your righteous acts have been revealed."

⁵ After this I looked, and I saw in heaven the temple—that is, the tabernacle of the covenant law—and it was opened. 6 Out of the temple came the seven angels with the seven plagues. They were dressed in clean, shining linen and wore golden sashes around their chests. 7 Then one of the four living creatures gave to the seven angels seven golden bowls filled with the wrath of God, who lives for ever and ever. 8 And the temple was filled with smoke from the glory of God and from his power, and no one could enter the temple until the seven plagues of the seven angels were completed.

Song of Moses

32 "Give ear, O heavens, and let me speak;
And let the earth hear the words of my mouth.

² "Let my teaching drop as the rain,
My speech distills as the dew,

As the droplets on the fresh grass
And as the showers on the herb.

3 "For I publish the name of the Lord;
Ascribe greatness to our God!

4 "The Rock! His work is perfect,
For all His ways are just;
A God of faithfulness and without injustice,
Righteous and upright is He.

5 "They have acted corruptly toward Him,
They are not His children, because of their defect;
But are a perverse and crooked generation.

6 "Do you thus repay the Lord,
O foolish and unwise people?
Is not He your Father who has bought you?

He has made you and established you.

7 "Remember the days of old,
Consider the years of all generations.
Ask your father, and he will inform you,
Your elders, and they will tell you.

8 "When the Most High gave the nations their inheritance,
When He separated the sons of Adam,
He set the boundaries of the peoples
According to the number of the sons of Israel.

9 "For the Lord's portion is His people;
Jacob is the lot of His inheritance.

10 "He found him in a desert land,
And in the howling waste of a wilderness;
He encircled him, He cared for him,
He guarded him as the pupil of His eye.

11 "Like an eagle that stirs up its nest,
That hovers over its young,
He spread His wings and caught them,
He carried them on His pinions.

¹² "The Lord alone guided him,
And there was no foreign god with him.

¹³ "He made him ride on the high places of the earth,
And he ate the produce of the field;
And He made him suck honey from the rock,
And oil from the flinty rock,

¹⁴ Curds of cows, and milk of the flock,
With fat of lambs,
And rams, the breed of Bashan, and goats,
With the finest of the wheat—
And of the blood of grapes you drank wine.

¹⁵ "But Jeshurun grew fat and kicked—
You are grown fat, thick, and sleek—
Then he forsook God who made him,
And scorned the Rock of his salvation.

¹⁶ "They made Him jealous with strange gods;
With abominations they provoked Him to anger

¹⁷ "They sacrificed to demons who were not God,
To gods whom they have not known,
New *gods* who came lately,
Whom your fathers did not dread.

¹⁸ "You neglected the Rock who begot you,
And forgot the God who gave you birth.

¹⁹ "The Lord saw *this* and spurned *them*
Because of the provocation of His sons and daughters.

²⁰ "Then He said, 'I will hide My face from them,
I will see what their end *shall be;*
For they are a perverse generation,
Sons in whom is no faithfulness.

²¹ 'They have made Me jealous with *what* is not God;
They have provoked Me to anger with their idols.
So, I will make them jealous with those *who* are not a people;
I will provoke them to anger with a foolish nation,

²² For a fire is kindled in My anger,
And burns to the lowest part of Sheol,
And consumes the earth with its yield,
And sets on fire the foundations of the mountains.

²³ 'I will heap misfortunes on them;
I will use My arrows on them.

²⁴ '*They will be* wasted by famine and consumed by plague
And bitter destruction;
And the teeth of beasts I will send upon them,
With the venom of crawling things of the dust.

²⁵ 'Outside the sword will bereave,
And inside terror—
Both young man and virgin,
The nursling with the man of gray hair.

²⁶ 'I would have said, "I will cut them to pieces,
I will remove the memory of them from men,"

²⁷ Had I not feared the provocation by the enemy,
That their adversaries would misjudge,
That they would say, "Our hand is triumphant,
And the Lord has not done all this."'

²⁸ "For they are a nation lacking in counsel,
And there is no understanding in them.

²⁹ "Would that they were wise, that they understood this,
That they would discern their future!

³⁰ "How could one chase a thousand,
And two put ten thousand to flight,
Unless their Rock had sold them,
And the Lord had given them up?

³¹ "Indeed their rock is not like our Rock,
Even our enemies themselves judge this.

³² "For their vine is from the vine of Sodom,
And from the fields of Gomorrah;
Their grapes are grapes of poison,

Their clusters, bitter.

33 "Their wine is the venom of serpents,
And the deadly poison of cobras.

34 'Is it not laid up in store with Me,
Sealed up in My treasuries?

35 'Vengeance is Mine, and retribution,
In due time their foot will slip;
For the day of their calamity is near,
And the impending things are hastening upon them.'

36 "For the Lord will vindicate His people,
And will have compassion on His servants,
When He sees that their strength is gone,
And there is none *remaining*, bond or free.

37 "And He will say, 'Where are their gods,
The rock in which they sought refuge?

38 'Who ate the fat of their sacrifices,
And drank the wine of their drink offering?
Let them rise up and help you,
Let them be your hiding place!

39 'See now that I, I am He,
And there is no God besides Me;
It is I who put to death and give life. I have wounded, and it is I who heal,
And there is no one who can deliver from My hand.

40 'Indeed, I lift up My hand to heaven,
And say, as I live forever,

41 If I sharpen My flashing sword,
And My hand takes hold on justice,
I will render vengeance on My adversaries,
And I will repay those who hate Me. (Atheists or unbelievers)

42 'I will make My arrows drunk with blood,
And My sword will devour flesh,
With the blood of the slain and the captives,
From the long-haired leaders of the enemy.'

⁴³ "Rejoice, O nations, with His people;
For He will avenge the blood of His servants,
And will render vengeance on His adversaries,
And will atone for His land and His people."

Song of Moses

The Author's Note:

This is the song of the overcomers who were not deceived. They have the seal of God in their minds and were protected from Satan's deceptions. They bear the gospel armor of God as their weapon to fight over the power of the enemy, who is Satan.

The Song of Moses has a strong message of warnings to the children of God. Moses predicted that after his death, which he had foreseen in their hearts, they would go astray. He spoke and reminded them of their past and the hard beginning they experienced in the wilderness. However, they were encouraged to continue with their lives with strong faith in God.

God gave the nations their lot, or domicile inheritances, and separated the races and made boundaries for each nation.

He found Jacob as his lot of inheritance in the growing wilderness. He blessed the place of their beginning and kept him as an apple of His eyes. He took care of the people like a mother eagle caring for her young with love, feeding, teaching, guiding, and giving them a good life. God is a perfect righteous God and was called the "Rock." While the Kenites are the offspring of Satan, who are corrupt in their ways and are a crooked generation, God provided His children with all the goodness: fruitful produce of the field, honey, oil, curds from the milk of the flocks, wheat, and pure wine from the vine of grapes. He made their lives safe and beautiful with all goodness of the field so that they were considered "over blessed." Then Jacob was given a name "Jeshuron," for he became thick and fat, well satisfied, but had forgotten his love for God who created him. God owned his soul, but now he turned his back on God and provoked Him to anger. God is a Jealous God. Jacob forsook God when he started listening and following the doctrines of false gods. He lost his faith in God by worshipping false gods and believed Satan's teachings of idolatry. He became unmindful of his love for God. God surely was sad and furious because God is a Jealous God. According to God, His anger is reserved for wrath at the end times. They will not escape from the pouring out of His cup of vengeance because He is also the Consuming Fire. He will scorch them with His burning fever that has no regard for anyone who is sinful in their ways. The cup of wrath that will be poured out will be disasters and calamities, famine, pestilences, which are painful and very destructive. This includes the bites of the beast, serpents, and scorpions as stated in His words of warnings.

The Kenites are enemies with no compassion. They don't care and have no understanding, lest they become wise and consider what things will happen and recognize the truth that there is a powerful God who is always open to repentance and forgiveness; therefore, there is hope for salvation. Our Rock has lots of compassion. Their rock is not our Rock. Their vine is the vine of Sodom and the fields of Gomorrah (who are perverse people). Their grapes are grapes of gall, their clusters are bitter, and their wine is the poison of dragons and the cruel venom of asps. Jesus had warned them in various places in the Bible.

> *"Vengeance is mine and recompense". (Deuteronomy 32:35)*

It will happen, for the Lord will judge His people and will have compassion on His servants (elect), who have a destiny to help put the enemy under His feet. He is always with them to strengthen and protect them.

> *"I am God and there is none besides me, says the Lord. I kill and make alive. I wound, and I heal. Nor is there anyone who can deliver from my hand". (Deuteronomy 32:39)*

His words from yesterday, today, and forever are the truth. He will hold judgment at the end of the millennium. He will avenge His children from the enemies and give reward to the worthy (the people He loves). Then He will provide atonement (reconciliation) for His land and His people.

Written 1400 BC

REVELATION CHAPTER 16
(From the Bible)

16 Then I heard a loud voice from the temple saying to the seven angels, "Go, pour out the seven bowls of God's wrath on the earth."

[2] The first angel went and poured out his bowl on the land, and ugly, festering sores broke out on the people who had the mark of the beast and worshiped its image.

[3] The second angel poured out his bowl on the sea, and it turned into blood like that of a dead person, and every living thing in the sea died.

[4] The third angel poured out his bowl on the rivers and springs of water, and they became blood. [5] Then I heard the angel in charge of the waters say:

"You are just in these judgments, O Holy One, you who are and who were;

[6] for they have shed the blood of your holy people and your prophets, and you have given them blood to drink as they deserve."

[7] And I heard the altar respond: "Yes, Lord God Almighty, true and just are your judgments."

[8] The fourth angel poured out his bowl on the sun, and the sun was allowed to scorch people with fire. [9] They were seared by the intense heat and they cursed the name of God, who had control over these plagues, but they refused to repent and glorify him.

[10] The fifth angel poured out his bowl on the throne of the beast, and its kingdom was plunged into darkness. People gnawed their tongues in agony [11] and cursed the God of heaven because of their pains and their sores, but they refused to repent of what they had done.

12 The sixth angel poured out his bowl on the great river Euphrates, and its water was dried up to prepare the way for the kings from the East.13 Then I saw three impure spirits that looked like frogs; they came out of the mouth of the dragon, out of the mouth of the beast and out of the mouth of the false prophet. 14 They are demonic spirits that perform signs, and they go out to the kings of the whole world, to gather them for the battle on the great day of God Almighty.

[15] "Look, I come like a thief! Blessed is the one who stays awake and remains clothed, so as not to go naked and be shamefully exposed."

[16] Then they gathered the kings together to the place that in Hebrew is called Armageddon.

[17] The seventh angel poured out his bowl into the air, and out of the temple came a loud voice from the throne, saying, "It is done!" [18] Then there came flashes of lightning, rumblings, peals of thunder and a severe earthquake. No earthquake like it has ever occurred since mankind has been on earth, so tremendous was the quake. [19] The great city split into three parts, and the cities of the nations collapsed. God remembered Babylon the Great and gave her the cup filled with the wine of the fury of his wrath. [20] Every island fled away, and the mountains could not be found. 21 From the sky huge hailstones, each weighing about a hundred pounds, fell on people. And they cursed God on account of the plague of hail because the plague was so terrible.

THE SEVEN VIALS (BOWLS)

AUTHOR'S NOTE:

As soon as the seventh trump sounds, all will be changed into spirit, and Jesus Christ will appear. Every knee will bow to Him, and Jesus will call on the four corners of the world to gather His elects, who are destined to teach with Him at the day of the millennium.

This is the wrath of God to be poured:

The seven vials are those wide-mouthed bowls in which the contents will splash.

Breaking the law will have consequences, in which men who disregard the Word of God will suffer. Here are the vials of wrath poured out by an angel with God's plague:

The first vial was poured on earth—loathsome and grievous sores come upon those who have the mark of the beast.

The second vial was poured on the sea—peoples and multitudes of tongues, nations, and races were killed (Revelation 17:15).

The third vial was poured on the rivers and springs of water—many people were killed. The waters that you saw where the harlot sits are peoples, multitudes, nations, and tongues.

The fourth vial was poured on the sun—men were scorched with fire (Word of God). Men scorched with great heat blasphemed the name of God and did not repent. This plague is very unique at the end times because it has power to produce a "burning" fever that will not withstand any attempt to heal.

The fifth vial was poured on the throne of the beast—his throne became full of darkness and with pain. From that source, people still ndid not repent.

*The sixth vial was poured on the great River Euphrates—its waters dried up. The river is between Israel and Babylon. So, people will have to choose which side they are on, between confusion with Satan, or God's truth. If people are learned with God's Word, they will stay faithful to God. Satan's kings are coming to deceive the whole world. These are the spirits of devils, the anti-Christ, the beast, and false prophets who used their weapons of fire, smoke, and brimstone.

All those cups of wrath poured out will not affect the believers of Christ because they stand firm on the Rock (Jesus), who protects them. The wrath is meant for the enemy. This plague was prayed about by Jesus to our Father to see if there was another way that salvation could be brought without the pouring out of His wrath, but His answer was "NO", so it must be done.

God sent His letter (The Bible) for us not to be deceived, as we were also forewarned repeatedly in many places in the Bible.

*The seventh vial was poured out into the air—a loud voice from heaven was heard. "It is done!" Then came a strong earthquake, noise, thunder, and lightning. That great earthquake was something unusually strong that never had occurred on earth before. Babylon was remembered before God to give her the cup of His fierceness of His wrath. Then, every mountain and island disappeared. A great hail fell upon men—each hailstone weighed about one hundred and ten to one hundred and eighty pounds. Men blasphemed God because of the great plague. All the cups of wrath poured out were very destructive and were meant to kill (spiritually). This is what He was saying about His vengeance on earth as forewarned.

REVELATION CHAPTER 17
(From the Bible)

17 One of the seven angels who had the seven bowls came and said to me, "Come, I will show you the punishment of the great prostitute, who sits by many waters. 2 With her the kings of the earth committed adultery, and the inhabitants of the earth were intoxicated with the wine of her adulteries."

³ Then the angel carried me away in the Spirit into a wilderness. There I saw a woman sitting on a scarlet beast that was covered with blasphemous names and had seven heads and ten horns. ⁴ The woman was dressed in purple and scarlet, and was glittering with gold, precious stones and pearls. She held a golden cup in her hand, filled with abominable things and the filth of her adulteries. ⁵ The name written on her forehead was a mystery:

BABYLON THE GREAT
THE MOTHER OF PROSTITUTES
AND OF THE ABOMINATIONS OF THE EARTH.

⁶ I saw that the woman was drunk with the blood of God's holy people, the blood of those who bore testimony to Jesus.

When I saw her, I was greatly astonished. ⁷ Then the angel said to me: "Why are you astonished? I will explain to you the mystery of the woman and of the beast she rides, which has the seven heads and ten horns. ⁸ The beast, which you saw, once was, now is not, and yet will come up out of the Abyss and go to its destruction. The inhabitants of the earth whose names have not been written in the book of life from the creation of the world will be astonished when they see the beast, because it once was, now is not, and yet will come. ⁹ "This calls for a mind with wisdom. The seven heads are seven hills on which the woman sits. ¹⁰ They are also seven kings. Five have fallen, one is, the other has not yet come; but when he does come, he must remain for only a little while. [11] The beast who once was, and now is not, is an eighth king. He belongs to the seven and is going to his destruction.

[12] "The ten horns you saw are ten kings who have not yet received a kingdom, but who for one hour will receive authority as kings along with the beast. [13] They have one purpose and will give their power and authority to the beast. [14] They will wage war against the Lamb, but the Lamb will triumph over them because He is Lord of lords and King of kings- and with Him will be called, chosen and faithful followers."

[15] Then the angel said to me, "The waters you saw, where the prostitute sits, are peoples, multitudes, nations and languages. [16] The beast and the ten horns you saw will hate the prostitute. They will bring her to ruin and leave her naked; they will eat her flesh and burn her with fire. [17] For God has put it into their hearts to accomplish His purpose by agreeing to hand over to the beast their royal authority, until God's words are fulfilled. [18] The woman you saw is the great city that rules over the kings of the earth."

AUTHOR'S NOTE:

Chapter seventeen is about the interpretation of God. However, we need to look at a little bit of history to be able to trace the sequences of seven nations that took part or were affected with the great deception that became widespread:

1. Babylon (Iraq)–during the time of Nebuchadnezzar

2. Medio (Iran)-Persia

3. Greece—Alexander

4. Rome—Caesar

5. Year AD 636 by the Mohammedans (Middle East)

6. The good and the bad figs (House of Israel)—The good basket of figs and the bad basket of figs returned to become a nation in 1948, was set up as a shoot, was planted, and has been growing to fulfill prophecies until the return of Jesu Christ.

7. Anti-Christ—Satan is the king of deception at the end times.**

An angel of God gave an explanation about the judgment of the great harlot. The harlot (Babylon) committed fornication with the earthly kings, and the people became drunk with her wine of fornication. The beast (Satan) on which she was sitting, having seven heads (nations) and ten horns (Satan's supernatural kings), was arrayed in a rich royal manner, purple and scarlet with gold and precious stones, and pearls, with a golden cup full of abominations and filthiness of her fornication. Her wine is the blood of the saints and martyrs of Jesus.

The Kenites (offspring of Satan), were responsible for the death of God's prophets, and the first murderer was Cain (the son of Satan).

**Dr. Arnold Murray Shepherd's Chapel CD vol. 2014 SCN #30284.08

"Therefore, you are witnesses against yourselves, that you are sons of those who murdered the prophets". "That on you may come all the righteous bloodshed on the earth". (Matthew 23:31-35)

On her head was written:

Mystery:

Babylon, the great, the mother of harlots and of the abominations of the earth.

The beast (Satan) that was, and is not, and yet is, will go to her (Apolliya—Satan's other name) perdition. He has already been judged long ago to perish (Ezekiel 28:18).

The seven beasts are seven mountains (nations) on which the woman sits floating on waters (peoples, nations, races, and tongues). There are also seven kings: five have fallen, one is, and the other has not yet come, and when he comes, he must continue a short time (five months). The beast that was, and is not, is himself also the eighth, and is of the seven (kings), who is going to perdition. Satan has multiple roles—here he is the 6th, 7th, and 8th king.

The ten horns are ten kings of Satan who are supernatural who have received no kingdom yet, but they will be given authority for one hour (hour of temptation, or five months) as kings with the beast. These are of one mind (to establish one world system) to govern the whole world.

These ten supernatural kings of Satan (fallen angels) will make war with the Lamb (Jesus Christ), and the Lamb will win with His chosen and faithful (elects). He is mighty, for He is the Lord of lords, and King of kings. They will hate the harlot and make her desolate and naked, eat her flesh, bring her to spiritual death of her soul, and burn her with fire.

For God has put it on their hearts to fulfill His purpose, to be of one mind, and to give their kingdom to the beast until the words of God are fulfilled. And the woman is the great city Babylon that reigns over the kings of the earth.

REVELATION CHAPTER 18
(From the Bible)

18 After this I saw another angel coming down from heaven. He had great authority, and the earth was illuminated by his splendor. 2 With a mighty voice he shouted:

"'Fallen! Fallen is Babylon the Great!'

She has become a dwelling for demons and a haunt for every impure spirit, a haunt for every unclean bird, a haunt for every unclean and detestable animal.

³ For all the nations have drunk the maddening wine of her adulteries.

The kings of the earth committed adultery with her, and the merchants of the earth grew rich from her excessive luxuries."

⁴ Then I heard another voice from heaven say:

"'Come out of her, my people,' so that you will not share in her sins, so that you will not receive any of her plagues;

⁵ for her sins are piled up to heaven, and God has remembered her crimes.

⁶ Give back to her as she has given; pay her back double for what she has done. Pour her a double portion from her own cup.

7 Give her as much torment and grief as the glory and luxury she gave herself. In her heart she boasts, 'I sit enthroned as queen. I am not a widow; I will never mourn.'

⁸ Therefore in one day her plagues will overtake her: death, mourning and famine. She will be consumed by fire, for mighty is the Lord God who judges her.

⁹ "When the kings of the earth who committed adultery with her and shared her luxury see the smoke of her burning, they will weep and mourn over her. 10 Terrified at her torment, they will stand far off and cry: "'Woe! Woe to you, great city, you mighty city of Babylon! In one hour your doom has come!' (5 months)

¹¹ "The merchants of the earth will weep and mourn over her because no one buys their cargoes anymore— ¹² cargoes of gold, silver, precious stones and pearls; fine linen, purple, silk and scarlet cloth; every sort of citron wood, and articles of every kind made of ivory, costly wood, bronze, iron and marble; ¹³ cargoes of cinnamon and spice, of incense, myrrh and frankincense, of wine and olive oil, of fine flour and wheat; cattle and sheep; horses and carriages; and human beings sold as slaves.

¹⁴ "They will say, 'The fruit you longed for is gone from you. All your luxury and splendor have vanished, never to be recovered.' ¹⁵ The merchants who sold these things and gained their wealth from her will stand far off, terrified at her torment. They will weep and mourn ¹⁶ and cry out:

"'Woe! Woe to you, great city, dressed in fine linen, purple and scarlet, and glittering with gold, precious stones and pearls!

¹⁷ In one hour such great wealth has been brought to ruin!' "Every sea captain, and all who travel by ship, the sailors, and all who earn their living from the sea, will stand far off. ¹⁸ When they see the smoke of her burning, they will exclaim, 'Was there ever a city like this great city?' ¹⁹ They will throw dust on their heads, and with weeping and mourning cry out:

"'Woe! Woe to you, great city, where all who had ships on the sea became rich through her wealth!

In one hour she has been brought to ruin!'

²⁰ "Rejoice over her, you heavens! Rejoice, you people of God! Rejoice, apostles and prophets!

For God has judged her with the judgment she imposed on you."

²¹ Then a mighty angel picked up a boulder the size of a large millstone and threw it into the sea, and said:

"With such violence the great city of Babylon will be thrown down, never to be found again.

²² The music of harpists and musicians, pipers and trumpeters, will never be heard in you again.

No worker of any trade will ever be found in you again.

The sound of a millstone will never be heard in you again.

²³ The light of a lamp will never shine in you again.

The voice of bridegroom and bride will never be heard in you again.

Your merchants were the world's important people. By your magic spell all the nations were led astray.

²⁴ In her was found the blood of prophets and of God's holy people, of all who have been slaughtered on the earth."

AUTHOR'S NOTE:

Babylon is that great city of confusion that became the habitation of demons and evil spirits. The angel from heaven cried, "*Babylon is fallen, is fallen.*" She is seen arrayed as a queen with the cup in her hand, which is the wine of wrath of her fornication with the kings of the earth that made them rich and live luxuriously. She is the harlot that sits on the beast (Satan) and is floating on waters (peoples, nations, races, tongues, and kings), as described in the book. She is so proud, saying, "*I sit as a queen and will not see sorrow. I am no widow.*" She used the four horns, the power of the one world system, to infiltrate and cause the problems coming from (see author's note in chapter 13):

- Political and governmental confusion.

- Financial manipulation.

- Education infiltrated by teaching lies by professors who mislead and confuse students.

- Religious. This is Satan's favorite topic because of teaching traditions of man, wrong doctrines, and falsehood.

Therefore, God will judge her for her many sins and wickedness in one day (The Day of the Lord) with death, mourning, and famine. God will burn her, for God is a Consuming Fire. Standing at a distance, the kings and the merchants of the earth will say, "*Her judgment has come.*" They will mourn over her, and they will lament to see the smoke of her burning. The ships of trade and commerce will be gone, and all precious and worldly goods will have no more value. God says, "Come out of her, my people!" (from confusion), for God says, "*Lest you share in her sins, and lest you receive of her plagues*" (Revelation 18:4).

God has avenged His holy apostles and prophets by burning her with violence, for that great city Babylon shall be thrown down from her sorcery.

From her sorcery, all the nations were deceived, and the blood of the prophets and saints were slain on earth by her.

SALVATION

Jesus Christ came on earth to become our savior. Apparently, God had planned this since the beginning of this earth age to fulfill His will.

Salvation is God's promise: "Indeed the Lord has proclaimed to the end of the world: say to the daughter of Zion, 'surely your salvation is coming: behold His reward is with Him and his work before Him. And they shall call them the Holy people, the Redeemed of the Lord: and you shall be called Sought Out, a City not Forsaken'" (Isaiah 62:11-12).

God's people, as promised will be judged and be given reward according to their righteous works.

A great multitude of all nations, tribes, peoples, and tongues were before the throne and before the Lamb, clothed in white robes, praising and worshipping God. These are the overcomers of the great tribulation who have washed their robes in the blood of the Lamb. They knew about God's truth and held on to it and were not deceived. The Lamb will feed and shepherd them, protect, and lead them to the living fountain of waters. God will wipe away every tear from their eyes (Revelation 7:17).

> *"Our God is the God of salvation, and to God belong escapes from death" (Psalm 68:20).*

God knows how to take care of His own people. He is not the God of the dead, but the God of the living. Nobody is truly dead yet except Satan who was already judged a long time ago. God gives life to deserving incorruptible souls and the mortal souls will be judged with the conscience of grace accordingly as shown in the book of life.

> *Sing to the Lord, all the earth, proclaim the good news of His salvation from day to day. (1 Chronicles 16:23)*

For the grace of God that brings salvation has appeared to all men, teaching us that, denying ungodliness and worldly lust, we should live soberly, righteously, and godly in the present age. (Titus 2:11)

REVELATION CHAPTER 19
(From the Bible)

19 After this I heard what sounded like the roar of a great multitude in heaven shouting: "Hallelujah!

Salvation and glory and power belong to our God,

For our Lord God Almighty reigns.

⁷ Let us rejoice and be glad and give him glory!

For the wedding of the Lamb has come, and his bride has made herself ready.

⁸ Fine linen, bright and clean, was given her to wear."

(Fine linen stands for the righteous acts of God's holy people.)

⁹ Then the angel said to me, "Write this: Blessed are those who are invited to the wedding supper of the Lamb!" And he added, "These are the true words of God."

¹⁰ At this I fell at his feet to worship him. But he said to me, "Don't do that! I am a fellow servant with you and with your brothers and sisters who hold to the testimony of Jesus. Worship God! For it is the Spirit of prophecy who bears testimony to Jesus."

¹¹ I saw heaven standing open and there before me was a white horse, whose rider is called Faithful and True. With justice he judges and wages war. ¹² His eyes are like blazing fire, and on his head are many crowns. He has a name written on him that no one knows but he himself. ¹³ He is dressed in a robe dipped in blood, and his name is the Word of God. ¹⁴ The armies of heaven were following him, riding on white horses and dressed in fine linen, white and clean. ¹⁵ Coming out of his mouth is a sharp sword with which to strike down the nations. "He will rule them with an iron scepter." He

treads the winepress of the fury of the wrath of God Almighty. [16] On his robe and on his thigh, he has this name written:

[17] And I saw an angel standing in the sun, who cried in a loud voice to all the birds flying in midair, "Come, gather together for the great supper of God, [18] so that you may eat the flesh of kings, generals, and the mighty, of horses and their riders, and the flesh of all people, free and slave, great and small."

19 Then I saw the beast and the kings of the earth and their armies gathered together to wage war against the rider on the horse and his army. 20 But the beast was captured, and with it the false prophet who had performed the signs on its behalf. With these signs he had deluded those who had received the mark of the beast and worshiped its image. The two of them were thrown alive into the fiery lake of burning sulfur.21 The rest were killed with the sword coming out of the mouth of the rider on the horse, and all the birds gorged themselves on their flesh.

AUTHOR'S NOTE:

A voice of multitude in heaven, the twenty-four elders, and the four living creatures were heard praising the Lord, saying "Hallelujah! Salvation, glory and power and honor to the Lord God, for He has avenged the blood of His servants, the holy apostles and prophets and all who were slain on earth." They were also heard saying:

"Rejoice for the marriage of the lamb has come in which she was granted to be arrayed with fine linen, clean and bright, for it is the righteous acts of the saints."

The angel said to John:

"Blessed are those who are called to the marriage supper of the Lamb. These are the true sayings of God."

John was taken back from the Lord's Day to AD 96. For all that he was shown and heard, he was so overwhelmed that he fell on his knees before the angel who had shown him everything in heaven as a testimony of Jesus. The angel said, "See that you do not do that! I am your fellow servant and of your brethren who have the testimony of Jesus. Worship God, for angel worship is a sin!" Our Almighty God is the Creator of everything. Nobody is above Him or can be greater than Him.

Then, I saw heaven opened and behold, a white horse and He who sat on him was called Faithful and True, and in righteousness, He judges and makes war.

"His eyes were like a flame of fire, and on His head were manycrowns, He had a name written that no one knows except Himself. He was clothed with a robe dipped in blood and His name is called the WORD of God." (Revelation 19:12-14)

He looked slain (He was crucified). And the armies in heaven, which were clothed in fine linen, white and clean, followed Him on white horses.

Now, out of His mouth goes a sharp sword, with which He strikes the nations with a rod of iron. He Himself treads the winepress of the fierceness of wrath of Almighty God, ready to execute vengeance. He has on His robe, and on His thigh, a name written:

KING OF KINGS AND LORD OF LORDS

And there, we also see Him as Melchizedek, chief priest of all religion forever. Many souls will have an opportunity to participate with Him at the millennium.

JESUS CHRIST AS MELCHIZEDEK

He had been with God all along since the beginning.

"In the beginning was the Word, and the Word was with God, and the Word was God" (John 1:1).

He is as it is written: without father or mother, without genealogy, having neither beginning of days nor end of life but made like the Son of God, who remains a priest continually. There is only one King of Righteousness and King of Peace. That is Jesus Christ. Melchizedek was the priest of the Most High God in the beginning. He met Abraham returning from the slaughter of kings and blessed him, and Abraham gave him a tent of all the spoils as tithe (Hebrew 7:1).

On one occasion when teaching a crowd of Jews, Jesus said, "Your father Abraham rejoiced to see my day, and he saw it and was glad" (John 8:56). Then the Jews said to Him, "You are not yet fifty years old, and have You seen Abraham?" "Most assuredly I say to you, before Abraham was, I Am" (John 8:58).

Then I saw an angel standing on the sun, and he cried with a loud voice, saying to all the birds that fly in the midst of heaven: "Come and gather together for the supper of the Great God, that you may eat the flesh of kings, the flesh of captains, the flesh of mighty men, the flesh of horses, and of those who sit, and the flesh of all people, free and slave, both small and great." (Revelation 19:17-18)

The flesh bodies are no more, for we are already in a different dimension (spiritual). "And I saw the beast, the kings of the earth, and their armies, gathered together to make war against Him who sat on the horse, and against His army.

Then the beast was captured and with him the false prophet who worked signs in his presence by which he deceives those who worshiped his image. These two were cast alive into the lake of fire burning with brimstone, and the rest were killed with the sword which proceeded from the mouth of Him who sat on the horse. And all the birds were filled with their flesh." (Revelation 19:19-21)

REVELATION CHAPTER 20
(From the Bible)

20 And I saw an angel coming down out of heaven, having the key to the Abyss and holding in his hand a great chain. 2 He seized the dragon, that ancient serpent, who is the devil, or Satan, and bound him for a thousand years. 3 He threw him into the Abyss, and locked and sealed it over him, to keep him from deceiving the nations anymore until the thousand years were ended. After that, he must be set free for a short time.

4 I saw thrones on which were seated those who had been given authority to judge. And I saw the souls of those who had been beheaded because of their testimony about Jesus and because of the word of God. They had not worshiped the beast or its image and had not received its mark on their foreheads or their hands. They came to life and reigned with Christ a thousand years. 5 (The rest of the dead did not come to life until the thousand years were ended.) This is the first resurrection. 6 Blessed and holy are those who share in the first resurrection. The second death has no power over them, but they will be priests of God and of Christ and will reign with him for a thousand years.

7 When the thousand years are over, Satan will be released from his prison 8 and will go out to deceive the nations in the four corners of the earth—Gog and Magog—and to gather them for battle. In number they are like the sand on the seashore. 9 They marched across the breadth of the earth and surrounded the camp of God's people, the city he loves. But fire came down from heaven and devoured them. 10 And the devil, who deceived them, was thrown into the lake of burning sulfur, where the beast and the false prophet had been thrown. They will be tormented day and night for ever and ever.

[11] Then I saw a great white throne and him who was seated on it. The earth and the heavens fled from his presence, and there was no place for them. [12] And I saw the dead, great and small, standing before the throne, and books were opened. Another book was opened, which is the book of life. The dead were judged according to what they had done as recorded in the books. [13] The sea gave up the dead that were in it, and death and Hades gave up the dead that were in them, and each person was judged according to what they had done. [14] Then death and Hades were thrown into the lake of fire. The lake of fire is the second death.[15] Anyone whose name was not found written in the book of life was thrown into the lake of fire.

THE MILLENNIUM

AUTHOR'S NOTE:

The millennium is the "Day of the Lord" (one thousand years).

"Behold, I tell you a mystery: we shall not all sleep, but we shall all be changed in a moment, in the twinkling of an eye at the <u>last trumpet</u>, our Lord Jesus Christ appears! For the trumpet will sound, and the dead will be raised incorruptible, and we shall be changed". (1 Corinthians 15:51)

All is changed into spiritual bodies. The elect are the faithful ones, chosen by God and destined to be with Jesus Christ to teach for one thousand years. All that were unlearned or those that are innocent of the knowledge of God will be under strict discipline.

The angel Michael, having the key of the bottomless pit, and a great chain in his hand, laid hold of Satan and bound him for one thousand years.

Satan will be locked up at the abyss for one thousand years with a special band so that he can no longer have any power to roam around.

Jesus Christ will rule and holds a rod of iron to strike the deceived nations as Lord of Lords and King of Kings as an avenger of our enemies. (Revelation 2:27)

The mystery of God is revealed after one thousand years. Satan will be released for a while for testing. Then judgment will follow at the end of the millennium, by the Godhead, Our Father.

One day to the Lord is like one thousand years (on earth) (2 Peter 3:8).

When we die, the spiritual body will step up from the flesh body and go back to God (Ecclesiastes 12:7). The spiritual souls can have a mortal or an immortal soul. Those dead flesh bodies are called corruptible bodies, and those who have spiritual souls, mortal and immortal, will be judged according to their works at the end of the millennium.

Their works are made of righteous acts that are woven to be worn to face judgment.

The souls that have the truth of God, and who have not worshipped the beast and his image (Satan), and have not received his mark on their forehead and hand, will be at the millennium with Jesus Christ and His elect to teach the unlearned. The second death has no power over them. The rest who did not make it in the first resurrection will have to wait till after one thousand years is over when Satan is released. Then, those who were taught will be tested. The test is necessary to find out those who have absorbed God's teachings. Those who still will not accept the truth will go into the lake of fire, while those who overcame will be judged according to their works (Revelation 20:13).

REMINDER:

We have two bodies (1 Corinthians 15:44):

1. The Natural or Terrestrial body (the flesh)—originally made of dust and is corruptible. The body that can decay or can become old, sick and die.

2. The Spiritual or Celestial body—we can have a mortal soul (liable to die) and/or immortal soul (deathlessness) that will be judged and can live eternally.

For this corruptible (flesh) must put on incorruption, and this mortal must put on immortality (1 Corinthians 15:53).

After one thousand years, when the Lord's Day is over, those who failed the test will be judged. Satan and his ten earthly kings will be gathered together at Mount Megiddo to battle (whose number is uncountable as the sand of the sea), surrounding the camp of the saints and the beloved city Jerusalem. Fire will come down from God and will kill them all. The devil will be cast into the lake of fire, where the beast and the false prophets are. They will be tormented day and night forever and ever, which surely means they shall be gone or finished and will not be remembered by anyone who is alive.

Meaning of Forever and Ever

Why does the wicked appear to be blessed and always ahead to achieve success? In Psalm 37:20, it is explained why the wicked seems to always be ahead and achieves success. God's answer:

"Rest in the Lord and wait patiently for Him. Do not fret because of him who prospers in his way. The wicked is like the fat of the lamb that drops the spit to the fire and smokes up to disappear forever and ever"

Also:

> *"Wait on the Lord and keep His way (Jesus is the way) and He shall exalt you to inherit the land and you are there to witness it". (Psalm 37:34)*

JUDGMENT TIME

Judgment has two parts:

1.   Final punishment, which is the death of the soul, and

2.   Reward of great blessings – this means life in eternity.

"At the great throne judgment, I saw the dead, small and great standing before God. There were books opened and another book was opened in which is the Book of Life. The dead were judged according to their works [works are the righteous acts of the saints]" (Revelation 20:12). The works are the things written in the book. We are sinners, and we fall short easily from righteousness, which is why repentance is very important. Repent! There should be a newness of heart (sincerity). All are judged according to their works. Righteous works are blessed with rewards, which overcome the unrighteous who are unworthy. Death and Hades were cast into the lake of fire. This is the second death, which is the death of the soul:

The fearful, unbelieving, abominable, murderers, sexually immoral, sorcerers, idolaters, and all liars shall have their part in the lake of fire, which burns with fire and brimstone.

This time, there will be no more lake. All, including the lake of fire, will be gone. The former heaven and earth had passed away.

Forever and ever has almost the same meaning as "blot out" by God when the unworthy souls are sentenced to the lake of fire. All memories of the living souls about them will be blotted out, not to be remembered at all (Revelation 20:14).

REVELATION CHAPTER 21
(From the Bible)

21 Then I saw "a new heaven and a new earth," for the first heaven and the first earth had passed away, and there was no longer any sea. ² I saw the Holy City, the new Jerusalem, coming down out of heaven from God, prepared as a bride beautifully dressed for her husband. ³ And I heard a loud voice from the throne saying, "Look! God's dwelling place is now among the people, and he will dwell with them. They will be his people, and God himself will be with them and be their God. ⁴ 'He will wipe every tear from their eyes. There will be no more death' or mourning or crying or pain, for the old order of things has passed away."

⁵ He who was seated on the throne said, "I am making everything new!" Then he said, "Write this down, for these words are trustworthy and true."

⁶ He said to me: "It is done. I am the Alpha and the Omega, the Beginning and the End. To the thirsty I will give water without cost from the spring of the water of life. ⁷ Those who are victorious will inherit all this, and I will be their God and they will be my children. ⁸ But the cowardly, the unbelieving, the vile, the murderers, the sexually immoral, those who practice magic arts, the idolaters and all liars—they will be consigned to the fiery lake of burning sulfur. This is the second death."

⁹ One of the seven angels who had the seven bowls full of the seven last plagues came and said to me, "Come, I will show you the bride, the wife of the Lamb." ¹⁰ And he carried me away in the Spirit to a mountain great and high, and showed me the Holy City, Jerusalem, coming down out of heaven from God. ¹¹ It shone with the glory of God, and its brilliance was like that of a very precious jewel, like a jasper, clear as crystal. ¹² It had a great, high wall with twelve gates, and with twelve angels at the gates. On the gates were written the names of the twelve tribes of Israel. ¹³ There were three

gates on the east, three on the north, three on the south and three on the west. [14] The wall of the city had twelve foundations, and on them were the names of the twelve apostles of the Lamb.

[15] The angel who talked with me had a measuring rod of gold to measure the city, its gates and its walls. [16] The city was laid out like a square, as long as it was wide. He measured the city with the rod Measured the city with the rod and found it to be 12,000 stadia in length, and as wide and high as it is long. [17] The angel measured the wall using human measurement, and it was 144 cubits thick. [18] The wall was made of jasper, and the city of pure gold, as pure as glass. [19] The foundations of the city walls were decorated with every kind of precious stone. The first foundation was jasper, the second sapphire, the third agate, the fourth emerald, [20] the fifth onyx, the sixth ruby, the seventh chrysolite, the eighth beryl, the ninth topaz, the tenth turquoise, the eleventh jacinth, and the twelfth amethyst. [21] The twelve gates were twelve pearls, each gate made of a single pearl. The great street of the city was of gold, as pure as transparent glass.

[22] I did not see a temple in the city, because the Lord God Almighty and the Lamb are its temple. [23] The city does not need the sun or the moon to shine on it, for the glory of God gives it light, and the Lamb is its lamp. [24] The nations will walk by its light, and the kings of the earth will bring their splendor into it. [25] On no day will its gates ever be shut, for there will be no night there. [26] The glory and honor of the nations will be brought into it. [27] Nothing impure will ever enter it, nor will anyone who does what is shameful or deceitful, but only those whose names are written in the Lamb's book of life.

The New Heaven and Earth

Author's Notes:

The new heaven and earth is portrayed as a beautiful and perfect sight. God's Holy City is here on earth in Jerusalem, rejuvenated and refreshed. All overcomers of God's judgment will enjoy eternal happiness in the new heavenly age, serving our Almighty God, and our precious Lord Jesus Christ. All lakes, including the lake of fire, are no more. There is no more sea.

John saw the Holy City, New Jerusalem, coming down out of heaven from God prepared as a bride (of Jesus Christ).

A loud voice from heaven was heard, "*Behold, the tabernacle of God is with men and He will dwell with them, and they shall be His people, God Himself will be their God.*"

God will wipe away every tear from their eyes: there will be no more death, nor sorrow, nor crying, no more pain.

God, who sits on the throne, said, "Behold, I make all things new." And He said to me, "*Write, for these words are true and faithful.*"

*"It is done! I am the Alpha and the Omega, the Beginning and the
End. I will give of the fountain of the water of life freely to him who
thirsts.*

*He who overcomes shall inherit all things, and I will be his God, and
he shall be my son [child, no gender]." (Revelation 21:6-7)*

*"And I heard a loud voice from heaven saying, "Behold, the tabernacle
of God is with men, and He will dwell with them, and they shall
be His people. God Himself will be with them and be their God."*
(Revelation 21:3)

The gender of people here is specifically mentioned in general, for men on earth.

The new Jerusalem will be the bride of Jesus Christ clothed with fine linen, clean
and white, which are the righteous acts of the saints.

Having the glory of God, the light was like a most precious stone, like a jasper
stone, clear as crystal. The city has a great high wall with twelve gates and twelve angels,
with names written are the twelve tribes of the children of Israel.

There are three gates on each side of a square.

The wall of the city had twelve foundations with the names of the twelve apostles
written on them.

The measurement of the city, laid out as a square, is twelve thousand furlongs. Its
length, breadth, and height are equal. The measurement of the wall was one hundred
forty-four cubits. The construction of the wall was of jasper, and the city was pure gold
like clear glass.

The foundations of the wall of the city were adorned with all kinds of precious
stones: jasper, sapphire, chalcedony, emerald, sardonyx, sardius, chrysolite, beryl,
topaz, chrysoprase, jacinth, and amethyst.

The twelve gates are twelve pearls. Each individual gate was of one pearl, and the
street of the city was pure gold. Nothing that defiles or causes abomination or utters
a lie can enter. No more sun, nor moon to shine. No night, no temple for the God
Almighty, because the Lamb is its temple. The glory of God illuminates the city, and
the Lamb is its light.

REMINDER:

When the first earth age was destroyed by God due to Satan's revolt (*katabole*), the
environment was disarrayed. This time, the old beautiful earth will return to its original
form. There will be no more storms or weather disturbances. The firmament will be
back to its original place protecting the earth and will have a comfortable temperature.

We know that prior to the judgment, at the end of the millennium, Jesus Christ had reigned to battle as a man of war. He fought and defeated death, who is Satan (Hebrew 2:14).

Revelation Chapter 22
(From the Bible)

22 Then the angel showed me the river of the water of life, as clear as crystal, flowing from the throne of God and of the Lamb ² down the middle of the great street of the city. On each side of the river stood the Tree of Life, bearing twelve crops of fruit, yielding of the nations. ³ No longer will there be any curse. The throne of God and of the Lamb will be in the city, and his servants will serve Him. ⁴ They will see His face, and His name will be on their foreheads. ⁵ There will be no more night. They will not need the light of a lamp or the light of the sun, for the Lord God will give them light. And they will reign for ever and ever.

⁶ The angel said to me, "These words are trustworthy and true. The Lord, the God who inspires the prophets, sent his angel to show his servants the things that must soon take place."

⁷ "Look, I am coming soon! Blessed is the one who keeps the words of the prophecy written in this scroll."

⁸ I, John, am the one who heard and saw these things. And when I had heard and seen them, I fell down to worship at the feet of the angel who had been showing them to me. ⁹ But he said to me, "Don't do that!

I am a fellow servant with you and with your fellow prophets and with all who keep the words of this scroll. Worship God!"

¹⁰ Then he told me, "Do not seal up the words of the prophecy of this scroll, because the time is near. ¹¹ Let the one who does wrong continue to do wrong; let the vile person continue to be vile; let the one who does right continue to do right; and let the holy person continue to be holy."

¹² "Look, I am coming soon! My reward is with me, and I will give to each person according to what they have done. ¹³ I am the Alpha and the Omega, the First and the Last, the Beginning and the End.

¹⁴ "Blessed are those who wash their robes, that they may have the right to the Tree of Life and may go through the gates into the city. ¹⁵ Outside are the dogs, those who practice magic arts, the sexually immoral, the murderers, the idolaters and everyone who loves and practices falsehood.

¹⁶ "I, Jesus, have sent my angel to give you this testimony for the churches. I am the Root and the Offspring of David, and the bright Morning Star."

¹⁷ The Spirit and the bride say, "Come!" And let the one who hears say, "Come!" Let the one who is thirsty come; and let the one who wishes take the free gift of the water of life.

¹⁸ I warn everyone who hears the words of the prophecy of this scroll: If anyone adds anything to them, God will add to that person the plagues described in this scroll. ¹⁹ And if anyone takes words away from this scroll of prophecy, God will take away from that person any share in the Tree of Life and in the Holy City, which are described in this scroll..

²⁰ He who testifies to these things says, "Yes, I am coming soon." Amen. Come, Lord Jesus.

²¹ The grace of the Lord Jesus be with God's people. Amen.

AUTHOR'S NOTES:

At the throne of God and the Lamb, all kinds of wickedness were burned at the lake of fire and were gone. Here, now, is the new heaven and earth with our Loving Almighty God with His overcomers. There was the spiritual water, clear as crystal, running down from the temple of God and the Lamb to form a river. On each side of the river was the Tree of Life (Jesus Christ), which bore twelve fruits, each tree yielding its fruit every month. The leaves of the tree were for medicine for healing of the nations (ethnos). In the middle of the street is the Tree of Life. There shall be no more curse, but the throne of God and the Lamb shall be in it. And His servants shall serve Him.

When we enter the Kingdom of God, we shall see His face, and His name shall be on our foreheads. We will know Him and will reign with Him forever and ever. In the eternal world with our Lord God, we partake of the fruit of the Tree of Life (Jesus Christ), from which its fruits and leaves are fulfilling and healing. This is divine feeding and healing, and that is why there is no unhappiness, boredom, or depression. Best of all, no more death.

"He who is unjust, let him be unjust, still, he who is filthy, let him be filthy still, he who is righteous, let him be righteous still: he who is holy, let him be holy still." (Rev 22:11)

REMINDER:

All we are required to do is plant a seed (teach the truth that is knowledge of God), and God will fertilize the seed and cause it to grow. Let them be as they are. It is up to God if they will be accepted. Almighty God is the judge, so leave the saving of the soul to God. He judges according to our works and, we will be given rewards according to our righteous acts.

"Behold, I am coming quickly, blessed is he who keeps the words of the prophecy of the book". (Revelation 22:7)

John was taken back from the millennium to the time AD 96. He was so overwhelmed with everything he saw and all he heard that he fell down to worship before the angel. He got carried away with himself. The angel prevented him and said, "See that you don't do that," and said, *"Worship God and do not seal the prophecy of this book, for the time is at hand."* Angel worship is a sin, for we are to worship only God. This book of Revelation is the message of God to be unveiled or revealed so that you will come to know and understand the chronological order of events that bring in the consummation of the age and for us not to be misled or deceived by our enemy who is Satan.

God brought forth His promise, of His plan of salvation, by giving men free will to love Him for blessings or to follow Satan. We must stay focused with our knowledge of God's truth to prevent deception and by wearing the gospel armor of God. We can stand with boldness on the Rock (Jesus Christ) and nothing will harm us.

The elects of God will work with the Holy Spirit by allowing Him to speak through them when they are delivered up to witness against the enemy, not to premeditate what to speak, but speak that what is given in that hour (hour of temptation) to allow the Holy Spirit to be heard by all people regardless of race, origin, even with any other tongue or language. And all will understand (Mark 13:11).

God said, *"And behold, I am coming quickly, and my reward is with Me to give according to his work. I am the Alpha and the Omega, the Beginning and the End, the First and the Last"* (Revelation 22:12-13).

Blessed are those who do His commandments, that they may have the right to the Tree of Life and may enter the gates into the city (the New Jerusalem). *"I Jesus, have sent my angel to testify these things in the churches, I am the Root and Offspring of David, the Bright and Morning Star"* (Revelation 22:16).

The kingdom of Almighty God and the Lamb is faithful and true, and the Holy Spirit and bride say, "Come." Jesus Christ says, "*Surely I am coming quickly.*" Amen. Even so, come, Lord Jesus!

The grace of our Lord Jesus Christ be with you all. Amen. "YHVH Shammah" (Yahovah Shammah). The Lord is where Life is Everlasting! (Ezekiel 48:35)*

BRIEF DESCRIPTIONS OF
MINOR PROPHETS:

1. Hosea—This name is almost like the name of "Yesuah," which means Jesus Christ (Yahoveh's Salvation, our Savior). Hosea, the prophet, who described his wife being as adulterous, is like a spiritually adulterous (wicked) nation because of idolatry and immorality. He urged them to return to God in order to be forgiven.

2. Joel—He illustrated the locust plague that attacked the land of southern Judah. The distress and sufferings from the locust devastation were likened to the coming of the Lord God. People need to repent with fasting and mourning to be forgiven of their sins.

3. Amos—He prophesied about unrighteousness of the northern part of Israel. He warned them of all their wickedness because they will be judged. They must repent and will finally be rewarded. He warned the people that the famine for the end times is not a famine of bread nor thirst of water, but hearing of the word of God.

4. Obadiah—The shortest book of the minor prophets. He tells about the arrogance and cruelty of the land of Edom called "Russia" today against Israel. It predicts the total destruction of the land of Edom.

5. Jonah—The book is a story about him who disobeyed God and was swallowed up by a large fish, but in the end, he was saved. God taught him a lesson that He is a God of compassion over all.

6. Micah – said "Who is like Yahoveh? No one". The people of the southern and northern kingdom of Israel were practicing false worship. This wickedness will also be present and seen in the future times before the end

of this age. They will also be judged. But, the coming of Jesus Christ will lead them, and they will be taught finally with the hope of salvation.

7. Nahum—He predicts the fall of Babylon, which portrays of battle with the enemy at end times.

8. Habakuk—This minor book also says that the wickedness of the land will be judged. He expressed praise of God's wisdom in a poem of thanksgiving and great faith.

9. Zephaniah— He reveals that the Day of the Lord is coming, and God will finally judge. The nation Judah must prepare for God's chastening wrath, yet salvation will follow.

10. Haggai—The message here is to put God first before the people's priorities with their personal affairs, which had caused them to neglect the rebuilding work of the temple in order to be blessed.

11. Zechariah— This book reminds the people that they are building not only a building, but establishing a future. This prophet's vision gives hope and comfort for the trying circumstances that will happen at the end times.

12. Malachi – God specifically warns false prophets that their way of teachings will be cursed.

So, all these minor books of prophecies are like reading messages of tomorrow's events to occur from God's words:

Jesus Christ is coming to rule nations, and repentance is necessary as a relief to obtain hope and forgiveness to show His mercy and compassion. There will be the great white throne of God to pronounce final judgment, either to protect you from plagues or cause you to suffer from them. If you overcome, you will receive your blessings for eternal salvation.

The book of Psalms is collection of Hebrew poetry. Most of the book contains praises about the Lord God and Jesus Christ.

The book of Proverbs is practical in everyday philosophy of life.

REVELATION
MEANING OF TERMS

1. Revelation: To unfold, to unveil, to reveal.

2. Apocalypse: Is the Greek word for Revelation.

3. Lamb: Means Jesus Christ as Lord of lords and King of kings.

4. Golden Lampstand: The Churches.

5. Stars: Angels or messengers of God.

6. Millennium: One day with the Lord is one thousand years to man on earth.

7. Seal: The knowledge of God's words, the truth.

8. Trumpets: The execution of command from God.

9. Vials (or bowls): A wide-mouthed cup with God's wrath to be poured out at the end of millennium.

10. Sword: The tongue of the Lord Jesus, with the twosided sharp edge, which cuts both ways to bring out truth (God's word).

11. "Works": The only thing that you can take with you (spiritually speaking) to heaven for judgment (e.g., the righteous acts of the saints).

12. Horn: It means power.

13. Mountain: Nations, countries, continents.

14. Waters: It means the peoples, multitudes, and tongues.

15. Hades: Hell, or the lake of fire at the end of the millennium after the great white throne judgment.

16. Beast: Satan's other name (also the son of perdition).

17. Anti-Christ: Instead of Christ.

18. Hour of temptation: Five months tribulation of Satan.

19. Fornication: Sexual perversion.

20. Elect: The chosen and faithful ones—set-aside ones during the foundation.

21. Wicked woman or that great city of confusion: Babylon.

22. Blot-out: To erase to be gone forever.

23. "Bride": The saints who will be married to Christ to become His wife in the new kingdom of God on earth (New Jerusalem).

24. Sorcery: Pharmacy, use of potions, medications by druggists, witchcraft.

GLOSSARY

A

Abominable—cursing, disgust, or hatred; cursed or condemnable.

Amber—highly polished bronze metal.

Amen—"That's that."

Anti-Christ—Instead of Christ.

Apocalypse—Is a Greek word for uncover or unveil.

Apostacy—Falling away. Abandonment of precious loyalty; defection from the truth.

B

Baal worship—False worship, idol worship.

Babylon—City of confusion.

Backsliding—To lapse morally, to depart from an acceptable standard. Also means defection.

Beast—Another name of Satan at the end of the age. A religious entity against God.

Beguiled—Wholly seduced.

Blasphemy—unpardonable sin, unforgivable; lack of reverence for God.

Blessings—God's favors of kindness, love, mercy, compassion, success, riches, and reward.

Blot—Erased forever gone; to erase from memory or the mind.

Bride—The saints or the elects, wife to be for Jesus.

C

Candlestick—Church lighting, symbolic of church.

Corruptible—Decay, reprove, rebuke.

Curse—The opposite of blessings; afflictions.

D

Damnation—For or against justice, to condemn.
Delusion—Deception, false belief.
Discern—To perceive to understand.
Doctrine—To bring, to carry, to pre-act, philosophy.

E

Elect—The righteous ones. The set-aside ones during the foundation of the world.
Enmity—Means hostility, eternal, forever.
Ethnos—The different races, tribes, nations, tongues.
Events—Seasons occurring in chronology.

F

Fallen angels—Wicked angels that seduced earthly women who bore giants (Gibor).
Foley—Foolish actions or conduct, evil, wickedness.
Fornication—Sexual perversion, deviation from normal; idolatry.

G

Generation—Bringing up offspring.
Gentiles—Of non-Jewish faith.
Golden lampstands—Churches.

H

Hades—Hell or the lake of fire.
Harlot—Sexual pervert, wicked woman.
Horn—power.
Hour of temptation—Five-month period of Satan on earth, or one hour in heaven.

I

Idolatry—worshipping images or idol worship, fornication.
Incorruption—Undefiled, immortal, deathlessness.
Immortality—To live forever.
Intercessory prayers—Prayer for someone.

J

Jealous—Envious feeling.

K

Katabole—Satan's rebellion in the first world, foundation age.

L

Labor—Works of righteous or unrighteousness.
Lamb—Jesus Christ.
Lie—No basis, untrue.
Longsuffering—Patience.

M

Manna—Corn of heaven, angel's food.
Millennium—One thousand years, the Lord's Day.
Mountain—Nation.
Morning Star—Jesus, our Lord (Satan claims he is).
Mortal—Liable to die.
Mystery—Hidden secrets.

N

Nation—Races, country, ethnic people, gentiles.
Nicolaitan Doctrine—Baal worship, false teaching, false philosophy.

O

One World System—Oneness of minds of nations.

P

Passover—Feast of the unleavened bread. Highest holiday of Christians.
Perdition—To be killed or destroyed. To disappear.
Perish—To destroy fully, to be killed.
Plague—Curses, disasters, calamities.
Priests—Somebody to preach or teach God's words.
Prophecy—Prediction of the future; Prophecies: all Jesus Christ's
prophecies are given in days. We are the children of light. Unlike all
prophecies given in moons are of Satan.
Posterity—Descendants or offspring.

R

Repentance—Full of regret that caused sin or sorrow.
Resurrection—To make to stand up, to raise from sleep, to awake
Revelation—To reveal, to uncover, to unveil.
Remnants—The remaining group of believers.
Rudiments—All evil things to be burned at the end of the age.

S

Sabbath—Rest day.

Seal—Knowledge of God in the mind.

Scribe—The writer.

Spirit—Invisible like wind.

Sorcery—Taken from the Greek word pharmakon, or druggist, or witchcraft.

Stars—Angels, the messengers of God.

Sword—The tongue of Jesus Christ with two sharp edges that cut falsehoods.

Symbolism—Use of symbols to mean something.

T

Tares—A weed of grain fields, bad grass.

Theory—Doctrine, belief.

Tree of Life – Jesus Christ

Tree of the knowledge of good and evil – Satan

Tribulation—period of distress or suffering resulting from oppression or persecution.

Transform—to disguise.

Trump—The execution of commands from God.

V

Veil—Curtain covering, veil over the head symbolizes Jesus Christ.

W

Waters—Peoples, nations, races, and tongues.

Wicked Woman—Babylon, the great city of confusion.

Word—Spoken by God. WORD is Jesus Christ.

Works—The righteous acts of the saints.

Wrath—God's fury in His cup to be poured out at the end times.

Y

Yahovah—Jehovah, pronounced (Ya-ho-vah), name of Almighty God, the Father in Hebrew.